Gita Wisdom

An Introduction to India's Essential Yoga Text

JOSHUA M. GREENE

Mandala Publishing
3160 Kerner Blvd., Unit 108
San Rafael, CA 94901
www.mandala.org
800.688.2218

MANDALA
PUBLISHING

Library of Congress Cataloging-in-Publication Data available.

ISBN-13: 978-1-60109-036-2

ROOTS of PEACE   REPLANTED PAPER

Roots of Peace is an internationally renowned humanitarian organization dedicated to eradicating landmines worldwide and converting war-torn lands into productive farms and wildlife habitats. Together, we will plant 2 million fruit and nut trees in Afghanistan and provide farmers there with the skills and support necessary for sustainable land use.

Printed in the United States by
Palace Press International.
www.palacepress.com

10 9 8 7 6 5 4 3 2 1

Gita Wisdom

An Introduction to India's Essential Yoga Text

JOSHUA M. GREENE

MANDALA
PUBLISHING
San Rafael, California

FOR KATU

TABLE OF CONTENTS

OVERVIEW

t is dawn, just before the start of an epic war. Two armies comprising nearly four million soldiers fill a vast battlefield. Warrior elephants, their armored tusks glistening in the sunlight, trumpet and stomp the ground. Horses tethered to gold-plated chariots pull at their reins, anxious for the attack. Soldiers beat drums, rattle spears, ready bows and arrows. Between the two armies, noble prince Arjuna looks out from his chariot and envisions the destruction to come. This war is a last chance for his family to regain the kingdom stolen from them fourteen years before by ruthless cousins. Yet, in these final moments, he falters. He turns to his friend and mentor Krishna, who serves as Arjuna's charioteer, and confesses to feelings of horror over the lives that will be lost and shame over his participation. What follows is a two-hour dialogue, known as the Bhagavad Gita, or "Song of the Supreme Person," one of the world's most renowned testimonies to the transformative power of love.

No voice recording exists of the conversation between Krishna and Arjuna. No audio file reveals which words were emphasized or delivered with greatest passion. No visual record survives to indicate facial expressions, gestures, body language, or other nonverbal indicators of intent and meaning. We are adrift in their discussion, charting our course by the celestial commentaries of wise yogis and learned devotees At the Gita's core, they declare, is this message: We have wandered away from our eternal self. Through practice of *bhakti*, the yoga of devotion, we can recover our lost identity as eternal beings and reawaken the love dormant in our souls. This, the Gita says, is the ultimate purpose of yoga and the fulfillment of the human mission.[1]

One devotee-scholar who dedicated his life to propagating this core message of the Gita was my teacher, His Divine Grace A.C. Bhaktivedanta Swami Prabhupada (1896–1977).[2] Prabhupada wrote an elaborate and well-known commentary titled *Bhagavad Gita As It Is*, but he believed that the Gita deserved the widest possible exposure and encouraged his students to publish their own realizations. What follows is an attempt to honor that mandate.

As with anything profound and beautiful, understanding of the Gita matures with time. When I began my bhakti studies at age nineteen, the Gita's warning about *kama* or "cravings" meant sex and food to me. Since then I have seen that intellectual pursuit, artis-

———————————————◈———————————————

[1] Scholarship places the composition of the Gita between 500 BCE and 200 CE and suggests that it took many centuries to reach its present form, each generation adding or subtracting textual content according to its needs. Through this reductive lens, some historians have come to view bhakti as a recent religious movement which draws upon earlier ideas to establish a more personal and humane social structure. Practitioners, on the other hand, favor the Gita's explanation of its origins as divine (4.1): God's own words delivered at the dawn of creation as a blueprint for humanity, rather than a historic reaction to political or economic conditions.

[2] I refer to my teacher hereafter by his honorific title Prabhupada, "the master at whose feet others gather."

Krishna with the gopis of Vraj.

tic expression, or scientific inquiry can also constitute a "craving" if it feeds pride and isolates us from our eternal self. When I was in my twenties *ahankara* or "ego" meant an independence which needed to be sublimated. Forty years later, I know the dangers of sublimation and can respect a healthy ego, one that is self-assured without being arrogant. Some of these modest realizations appear here in the form of footnotes. Since this book is also intended to familiarize readers with many of the Gita's main concepts and terms, these have been indicated in *italics* upon their first appearance in the text. The most prevalent of these are explained in the chapter titled "Topics in the Gita."

The word "Bhagavad" in the title refers to Krishna, a name used in India's bhakti texts to indicate God in personal form. Within the context of the Gita, "God" and "Krishna" are basically the same, with one important distinction: God refers to the Supreme Being with reference to a creative function, while Krishna refers to the individual behind that creative function—a unique individual possessing a beautiful form and loving demeanor.[3] The name Krishna translates as "most attractive," and for thousands of years Krishna's attractive, loving nature has inspired expressions of devotion in art, poetry, music, and dance. Bhakti scholars describe the soul's yearning to love God as occuring in progressive stages called *rasas*, or tastes, rising from a passive awareness to servitude, friendship, parental affection and, in its most intense form, a mood of conjugal intimacy. The Bhagavata Purana offers a description of this love for the Supreme in its highest stage:

> *"Hearing the sweet music of Krishna's flute the hearts of the* gopis *[cowherd women] melted, their passion swelled, and with earrings swinging wildly they ran to the place where their beloved waited. He is the Supreme Soul, but they knew him only as their lover. He is imperishable, the origin of creation, yet he appears in the world to receive the love of his devotees. The gopis said, 'O dear one, please quench the fire burning in our hearts with the nectar of your lips. Who in all the worlds would not abandon everything for you? Even animals, trees, birds and cows are elated seeing your beauty. . . .'"* [4]

---

[3] See, for example, 9.11.

[4] This is summarized from Bhagavata Purana, Book 10, Chapter 29. Descriptions of the soul's yearning to love God with intimate intensity appear in many faith cultures. See for instance the writings of Sufi poet Rumi.

The Bhagavata says that this Krishna who plays sweet music and attracts the hearts of all souls is the ultimate object of love. In the Gita he fulfills a more sober role, that of Supreme Person appearing in the world to reestablish *dharma*, or the path of righteousness. Starting in the 1700s when they entered India, British educators and missionaries differentiated these two sides of Krishna's personality for reasons we will explore later.[5] Yet to achieve a clear understanding of the Gita, readers should remember that Krishna the beloved of all souls and Krishna the Supreme Being and upholder of dharma are one and the same individual.

According to Gita theology, all souls emanate from the Supreme Being and share his loving nature, as sparks emanating from a fire share in minute degree the fire's heat and light. This includes the Supreme Being's independence. Love implies possessing the independence to not love, and some souls leave their relationship with the Supreme Being to experience life apart in the material world. Over countless births, layers of psychic conditioning cover remembrance of their original nature and the hearts of these forgetful or "conditioned" souls grow hard. Krishna's purpose in speaking the Gita was to reveal how hard hearts can be softened through bhakti. Because the Gita touches on many topics, the majority of commentaries (there are more than 400 in English alone) miss this message of love in their philosophical and religious analyses, yet it is the core of the Gita's instruction.

Not everyone confronts enemies on a literal battlefield as Arjuna does in the Gita; still, the Gita poses questions which challenge us all: Who are we? Where do we come

---

[5] See footnote 94, p. 43.

◗ RIGHT: *Krishna the cowherd and Krishna speaker of the Gita are one and the same Supreme Person.* ◖

from? Why we are here? And, as with all great literature, the more we study the Gita's main characters, the more they resonate with emotions we can understand. Krishna and Arjuna played together as children. They were close friends in youth and became family when Arjuna married Krishna's sister. We learn from other bhakti texts that later in life they shared extraordinary adventures, including a journey through subtle pathways to places outside the known universe. Plainly put, India's most revered scripture is a heart-to-heart talk between two people bound together by friendship and love.[6]

Krishna and Arjuna's love for one another pervades the Gita. More than once Krishna tells Arjuna he chose him above all others to receive the Gita's wisdom because of this love. It was an odd choice, given the profile of people to whom God usually speaks. Arjuna was not among the religious elite of his day. He was not a scholar or mystic yogi. No shooting stars at birth foretold that he would be a prophet later in life. Prior to the battle of Kurukshetra he showed no inclination toward the kind of renunciation or austerity which often precedes profound visions. Arjuna was a military officer and family man whose main qualification for receiving "the most secret of all secrets"[7] was being Krishna's good friend and devotee. His love

---

[6] The Gita constitutes seven hundred verses in the one hundred thousand-verse epic history Mahabharata, which offers details of the circumstances before, during, and after the eighteen-day Kurukshetra war and of Krishna and Arjuna's relationship. See appendix for recommended editions.

[7] Krishna uses this phrase to describe the inner meaning of the Gita in 9.2.

Arjuna accepts Krishna as his guru.

for Krishna was all he needed to receive his message for humanity. And, as we shall see, that message is a call for all souls to rejoin him in bhakti, the yoga of loving devotional service.[8]

The Bhagavad Gita unfolds like a two-character play. We, the audience, watch as Krishna conducts Arjuna's chariot between their army and the army of their ene-

---

[8] Souls share a variety of loving relationships with Krishna. These are briefly described under *rasa* in "Topics in the Gita."

mies. We hear Arjuna describe his horror on seeing that among the people he must kill are former teachers and respected elders. We listen to his reasons for not wanting to kill them. We witness his deterioration into paralysis and watch as Krishna guides Arjuna out of his confusion with teachings on how to live an enlightened life. We share with Arjuna a never-before-seen vision of Krishna's divinity. We observe Arjuna's transformation at the conclusion of their talk; and we are there when an invigorated Arjuna stands up ready to lead his army to victory.

This call to action is one of the Gita's main teachings. Boiled down to its essence, the Gita says that all beings are eternal souls distinct from their bodies and minds. Because they have lost all conscious awareness of their immortal selves, people act in selfish ways that extend their imprisonment in material bodies. By acting with bhakti, or the yoga of love, conditioned souls can reawaken their eternal self and end the cycle of rebirth.

That is more or less everything, and the rest of Krishna's talk with Arjuna covers subjects that reinforce these basic points. It is a timeless, exquisite text. Read and be inspired.

A NOTE ABOUT THE TRANSLATION

My Gita studies began in 1969 at the London Radha Krishna Temple. Starting in 1973, I traveled with my teacher Prabhupada on his many tours across Europe. When I was asked to serve as editor of his books in European editions, we frequently met to discuss points of philosophy. I was struck by how receptive he was to using contemporary idioms to convey millennial teachings. On one occasion, we discussed art and beauty. "Beauty gratifies the eye," he said. "Art is different. Spiritually, art means service to God." I mentioned artist Andy Warhol who made art by taking things out of context, such as a soup can. "Maybe you call it art, " Prabhupada said with a smile, "but so far as the Gita is concerned, art means an offering of love to God." Many such discussions with Prabhupada prompted me to use contemporary references in *Gita Wisdom*.

Classic and modern translations of the Gita have their particular merits, and I consulted several in preparing the summary verses offered here. Obviously, this book was undertaken as a popular rather than scholarly work, and readers might wish to consult the recommended editions listed at the back for a more comprehensive look at the Gita's beautiful verses. *Gita Wisdom* is a non-technical abridgement that clusters and paraphrases verses to convey their general sense.[9] Its purpose is to present

Krishna and Arjuna as real persons and to provide a concise introduction to their talk in contemporary language.[10] Here is one of the greatest wisdom texts of all time; it speaks to every one of us, and what it says deserves to be portrayed in a contemporary vernacular. Still, some verses have been left out, either to avoid repetition or condense the telling, and I accept responsibility for any misrepresentation that may have resulted.

The verses appear in nonsexist language, respecting Krishna's declaration (9.32 and elsewhere) that he makes no distinction among souls. Masculine nouns consequently appear either plural ("persons who") or neutral ("such a soul" or "such a person"). Krishna uses a dozen different names for Arjuna, and Arjuna uses more than twenty names for Krishna. Only the names Krishna and Arjuna have been used, although titles such as "Supreme Person," "Supreme Soul," and "Supreme Being" occur as synonyms for Krishna. Terms such as *atma*, *brahman*, *karma*, and *guna* have been kept in Sanskrit since they defy simple English equivalents. Definitions for these are offered in the chapter "Topics in the Gita."

---

[9] An example of this clustering appears in Chapter 6. Verses 24 to 33 form a succinct description of the path to becoming a "highest yogi." They appear as a single entry in *Gita Wisdom*.

[10] In the words of Aldous Huxley, "Our eternal life, now and hereafter, stands in the knowledge of God; and this knowledge is not discursive but of the heart, a super-rational intuition, direct, synthetic, and timeless." (From the introduction to *The Song of God: Bhagavad-Gita*, translated by Swami Prabhavananda and Christopher Isherwood, New York: New American Library, 1944)

For generations, the Bhagavad Gita was carefully preserved and transmitted by realized sages. Well, Google put an end to that. Key in the right phrase and you can access a whole 7-Eleven of oversimplified editions. Sadly, consumer culture has appropriated the Gita and turned it into a product for the yoga market, and writing this brief book obliged me to confront that dilemma. Would I be part of the problem by presenting an abridged introduction to this sacred text? Then I remembered Krishna's words: "Even a leaf or a little water offered sincerely will be accepted."

And so, according to tradition and with whatever sincerity I have at my disposal, I ask for the blessings of my spiritual master and the community of devotees that this modest effort may inspire in readers an appreciation for their own divinity and the love that unites them with Krishna.

Bhagavad Gita Summary Verses

1

he sage credited with first committing the Gita to written form, Vyasadeva, knew how to involve people in a philosophical discussion: Emphasize the action-adventure story taking place around it. Chapter 1 sets the scene[11] beginning with blind king Dhritarashtra,[12] father to the malevolent Kauravas, asking his minister, Sanjaya, to engage psychic skills to relate what is happening on the battlefield. In this first section we also meet the main characters and witness the dilemma that must be resolved, namely Arjuna's refusal to fight.

1.1 Dhritarashtra asked, "On the sacred battlefield Kurukshetra, how did my sons and the sons of Pandu act?"[13]

---

[11] The Gita is a dialogue, not a book, and did not originally have chapters. Over time, commentators added chapter breaks to mark shifts in the discussion.

[12] Due to his ambition, Dhritarashtra was blind spiritually as well as materially. From their childhood, he fostered in his sons a lethal envy of their cousins the Pandavas.

[13] The more frequent translation is, "What did they do?" Yet as described by Graham Schweig in *The Beloved Lord's Secret Love Song*" (Harper San Francisco, 2007, p. 21), it is how we

2 GITA WISDOM *An Introduction to India's Essential Yoga Text*

1.2–13 Sanjaya answered, "Your sons rallied their troops, announcing the mighty warriors by name. Those warriors sounded their battle cry with drums, horns and conches[14] and the sound was tumultuous.

1.14–19 "Krishna and Arjuna's soldiers replied with their conches, creating an overwhelming vibration that filled the earth and sky. When heard by your sons, it shattered their hearts.[15]

1.20–23 "Arjuna prepared to signal the start of battle, then stopped and requested Krishna to draw his chariot up between the armies to better assess the opposing forces.[16]

---

behave rather than what we do which ranks as a main theme in the Gita. The king's inquiry speaks as much to the integrity of the armies as to their physical actions.

[14] In India, it is said that blowing through a conch makes the sound OM (also spelled AUM), the primal vibration that set creation in motion.

[15] Sanjaya is intimating to Dhritarashtra that his sons intuitively understood they could not win a war waged against the righteous Pandavas, particularly since Krishna was on their side.

[16] It is significant that Krishna plays a subservient role as charioteer to his devotee-friend Arjuna. Krishna presents himself in the Gita as God in personal form, but one of his many other names is *bhakta-vatsala*, meaning controlled by the love of his devotees.

1.24–28 "Krishna complied, and Arjuna gazed on the enemy: teachers and family, friends and relatives. Overwhelmed by compassion he then spoke."[17]

1.29–30 Arjuna said, "Krishna, I see familiar faces here, honorable men ready to fight and die. My mouth has gone dry. I tremble, perspire, my skin burns, and I can no longer hold my bow.[18] I do not remember who I am. I see only horror before me.

1.31–45 "No good can come from this. I could not live with victory. Even though they wish me harm, I am unwilling to kill family or friends. The Vedas say there is only sin in a deed that would undermine the kingdom. The wrong in such killing is inescapable: destruction of tradition, orphaned children—better that my enemies kill me first."[19]

1.46 Arjuna threw down his bow and arrows and collapsed on his chariot, weeping.[20]

---

[17] From this point on the Gita unfolds as a running dialogue between Krishna and Arjuna, although technically we are getting the account from Sanjaya.

[18] Arjuna's dilemma is real and, as Gita scholar J.A.B. van Buitenen points out, "an honorable one" (*The Bhagavadgita in the Mahabharata*, University of Chicago Press, 1981, p. 3). Among those whom he must kill are his grandfather Bhishma, revered guru and eldest member of Arjuna's family, and Arjuna's military instructor Dronacharya, his mentor since childhood.

Contemplating the horrors of war, Arjuna refuses to fight.

---

[19] This is an admittedly abridged recounting of Arjuna's various arguments for not fighting, which include ethical, strategic, religious, cultural, and personal excuses. Krishna addresses these throughout the Gita, in effect turning each argument on its head by redefining its terms.

[20] Some commentators suggest that an accomplished warrior such as Arjuna would not have been bewildered by a military challenge, however difficult. His collapse on the verge of battle, they propose, must have been divinely arranged so that the Gita could be spoken for the benefit of humanity.

*K*rishna reminds Arjuna of a tenet fundamental to all yoga practices: The true self or soul (atma) is different from its external body-mind vehicle. Embracing this vision of the soul's immortality builds the psychic strength needed to confront challenges without fear. And that, Krishna says, is one of the characteristics of advanced yogis, along with control of lower impulses, selfless commitment to doing the right thing, compassion for others, and inner peace.

2.1 Sanjaya said, "Arjuna was overwhelmed by compassion and his eyes filled with tears."[21]

2.2–3 Krishna said, "This is an hour of crisis. Why such weakness of heart? This does not become a noble-minded *Aryan*.[22] It is inappropriate. Stand up."[23]

---

[21] Tears can signal openness to dramatic change. If Arjuna had not been prepared for change, he would have left the battlefield. Instead he stayed, knowing he would have to confront his worst fear. The compassionate tears were as much for himself as for those whom he would destroy. The message of the Gita is that each of us confronts crisis and each of us is equipped with tools for moving past it.

[22] This word literally translates as "noble" or "honorable," i.e., persons who know the true value of life. The term *Aryan* was

2.4–6 Arjuna said, "Do you not see here my grandfather, my martial arts guru, and others who merit my respect? If we win at the cost of their lives, everything I touch will be tainted with blood. Better to live from begging—or better still, let them kill me first.

---

appropriated by early twentieth-century European racial theorists to identify "a noble race" descended from an ancient people of superior stock. "Aryan-Nordic" descendants by this definition were racially superior, a bizarre conclusion concocted from bits of history and genetics, which situated "pure-blood Germans" at the top of the evolutionary ladder and relegated other human groupings below them, thus rationalizing Nazi anti-Semitism. Because of its racist connotation, the term is usually avoided in Gita translations.

[23] Judged by its storyline, the Gita seems to reinforce post-9/11 pessimism about our ability to resolve disagreements with anything other than violence. Historically as well, there has been confusion over a wisdom text that exalts *ahimsa*, or nonviolence, yet concludes with war. The apparent contradiction is resolved when we recognize the righteousenss of the Pandavas' cause and how much effort they made to avoid bloodshed. The Kauravas were a murderous clan that usurped the Pandava kingdom by criminal actions and devious political maneuvers. This left the Pandavas few nonmilitary options, all of which were quickly exhausted: negotiation, compromise, diplomacy, appeals to reason and promises of immunity, all to no avail. In a final attempt to avoid violence, the five Pandava brothers petitioned the Kauravas for one village each, a concession which would have allowed them to retain a modicum of dignity. The Kauravas were adamant and refused to grant "even land enough in which to drive a pin."

2.7–9 "I am weak, Krishna, and confused about my dharma. Help me. Now I am your disciple.[24] Please instruct me. I will not fight."

2.10–12 Krishna smiled and said, "You talk like a learned man but mourn for what is not worth mourning. You, me, all these warriors—never was there a time when we did not exist, nor will we ever cease being.[25]

2.13–17 "The soul within the body passes from childhood to old age and then into another body at death. In the course of a life, happiness and distress come and go

———————————————— ❁ ————————————————

At that point, war was inevitable. The Gita does not sanction violence, but neither does it sanction cowardice when action is required for a righteous cause.

[24] Arjuna presents himself to Krishna as a disciple, in effect saying he wishes to set aside their friendship for the purpose of receiving formal instruction at a time when it is critically needed. The guru-disciple relationship is addressed again in 4.34-35.

[25] Krishna is not condemning Arjuna for being compassionate, a quality that the Gita glorifies as noble and indicative of developed human character. His point is that in this instance Arjuna's compassion is misplaced on two counts: first, due to their criminal behavior the Kauravas had lost the right to Arjuna's respect; and second, life is not permanently lost as will be explained in the following verses. Also important here is the implication that Krishna, Arjuna, and all the assembled kings exist eternally as distinct entities, refuting the notion popular among monistic schools of philosophy that individuality is an illusion.

"If I am to be reborn," prays Bhakti poet Raskhan (1533-1588), "let it be as one of your cowherds." The soul, Krishna assures Arjuna, never dies.

like the seasons. They are mere sensory impressions, Arjuna. Do not be disturbed by such impermanence. You, the soul within the body, endure and cannot be destroyed. Nothing can touch the imperishable soul.

2.18–24 "Material bodies will all perish. Fight, Arjuna, for the soul is unborn and immortal. Death is but a change of clothing. The self within the body cannot be cut by weapons, burned by fire, drenched by water, withered by wind. You are eternal, unbreakable, and ever the same.[26]

2.25–31 "Do not grieve for the loss of the body or the rebirth of the soul. You are a warrior fighting a just cause. There is no need to hesitate.[27]

2.32–41 "Be glad for this opportunity to execute your duty as a warrior. If you do not, you will lose your reputation and be dishonored. Your cowardice will forever be remembered—an infamy worse than death. Fight, without considering consequences to yourself, without considering victory or defeat. Die here and enter heaven, or win victory and regain your kingdom. There is no loss and

---

[26] Knowing ourselves to be "eternal" and "unbreakable" generates extraordinary physical and psychic strength. At age eighty, my teacher Prabhupada could do more in a day than ten people half his age. The body may grow old and weary, but the soul never ages. While quite small, the soul is described in the Sanskrit texts as the equivalent of ten thousand suns: an ever-vibrant atomic core which can provide vast amounts of energy.

[27] On the one hand, a soldier cannot afford to let compassion interfere with fighting a righteous battle; and in these early moments of their discussion Krishna reminds Arjuna to set his gentler self aside for the sake of what he must do. On the other hand, being a soldier is not Arjuna's eternal identity, and later (12.9-19) Krishna will praise qualities of enlightenment such as compassion and equality toward friends and enemies alike. In effect, Krishna is telling Arjuna that, for now, he must direct his compassion away from the Kauravas and toward victims of their despotic rule. The Sanskrit word for warrior,

only gain for those of firm determination who embark on this path of dharma. They are resolute in purpose, single-minded, and their intelligence never waivers.

2.42–46 "The naive quote flowery words of scripture, for they seek heavenly rewards;[28] but the Vedas pertain to the material *gunas*[29] Rise above the gunas, Arjuna, for you have a higher purpose that fulfills all scriptural teachings, just as the purpose of small wells is served by a great reservoir of water.

2.47–53 "Perform your duty, for that is your right, but do not covet its fruits. Act with equanimity. That is the way of yoga, the art of all work. Great sages have gone beyond birth and death by such selfless action.[30] Inure

---

kshatriya, means "one who protects others from harm." The implication is that, under justifiable circumstances, a warrior's use of force is *ahimsa*, or non-aggression.

[28] Krishna is chastising Arjuna for having quoted scripture (1.31–45) to justify his refusal to fight. This is less a condemnation of scripture than a warning to Arjuna not to miss the forest for the trees. Rituals and heavenly rewards may have their place, but an intelligent person such as Arjuna should arrive at a deeper sense of scriptural purpose.

[29] See "Topics in the Gita."

[30] Several times in the Gita, Krishna refers to teachers, sages, and sacred texts to substantiate his message to Arjuna. These three sources—*guru*, *sadhu*, and *shastra*—are the check-and-balance system which validates wisdom in traditional yoga culture. *Gurus* do not concoct teachings but cite *shastras*, or revealed texts, to substantiate their lessons; and because scrip-

yourself to scriptural promises and fix your mind on the Self within.[31] This state of *samadhi*[32] is the goal of yoga."

2.54 Arjuna asked, "What is the behavior of those who live in such yogic consciousness?[33] How do they speak and sit and move?"

2.55–59 Krishna said, "Their minds are steady and calm.[34] They are free from fear and anger, unaffected by good and evil. They deploy their senses only when needed as a tortoise does its limbs. Yogis transcend the life of the senses, for they know a higher taste.

---

tures are subject to interpretation, commentaries by *sadhus* or sages are as critical as the scriptures themselves.

[31] The majority of world scriptures (including the ancient Indian Vedas to which Krishna alludes here) advise people how to live a moral, prosperous life in the external world. The word *nirvedam* in 2.52, "indifferent" or "inured," is quite possibly a bit of Krishna humor, the punning of a word which could also mean "Veda-less."

[32] See "Topics in the Gita."

[33] The word yoga or words related to it occur more than 150 times in the Gita, underlining the Gita's preeminence among guides to yoga practice.

[34] Of all the benefits available through yoga, a steady and calm mind is the first and most fundamental, without which higher levels are difficult to attain.

[35] This is the first time Krishna introduces himself as the goal of yoga, a theme he will emphasize throughout the dialogue.

2.60–61 "The senses are strong and impetuous and carry away the mind even of those endeavoring to control them, but by exercising self-control and meditating upon me you will achieve steadiness.[35]

2.62–63 "Those who contemplate the cravings of the senses become attached to having them.[36] Attachment breeds lust. Lust leads to anger, and from anger delusion arises. Delusion bewilders memory.[37] When memory is bewildered intelligence is lost, and from there one falls into complete madness.

---

[36] Krishna seems ambiguous about certain topics, a concern Arjuna raises at the start of the next chapter. Here, for instance, cravings or desires are branded as enemies of those seeking to know their higher self, yet Krishna encourages Arjuna's desire to fight with visions of heavenly and earthly rewards. As we proceed through the dialogue, we will see that bhakti is not a path of self-denial. The soul is by nature pleasure-seeking, and desire is not in itself wrong (3.6–9). The Gita distinguishes between selfish, hurtful desires—cravings that are appeased at the expense of others—and healthy desires which are not destructive to ourselves or to others and which result in benefit for all. Krishna's admonition about unbridled cravings is an expression of his concern that we not let them get the better of us (3.37–41).

[37] The memory referenced here could be understood as memory of past mistakes. Ideally, we learn by our mistakes, but letting the mind dwell too long on a selfish desire erases the lessons we should have learned from prior experience.

2.64–68 "Even one of the senses can carry away the mind of an intelligent person, but by practicing yoga with a full heart one obtains divine grace.[38] And by such grace, those with steady intelligence live free from material misery. Without such intelligence and grace there can be no peace. For even one of the senses can carry away intelligence, just as a strong wind may carry away a boat on the water.

2.69–72 "What is night for the rest of the world is day for those absorbed in yoga. And when the world is awake, that is night for the introspective sages who are like the ocean, which is ever still despite the constant influx of river waters.[39] They have divested themselves of ownership and ego, and they alone attain true peace. Those who maintain such consciousness at the end of life attain peace everlasting."

---

[38] *Prasadam* translates as grace or mercy and also food sanctified with prayer.

[39] Both metaphorically and literally, yogis are awake while others sleep. The most effective time for meditation is early morning. The *brahma-muhurta* or "auspicious time of *brahman*" is the forty-eight minutes just prior to sunrise. Prayer, meditation and other contemplative exercises are particularly powerful then and put the rest of the day in proper perspective. See *brahman* in "Topics in the Gita" for a detailed definition of the word.

3

ne way to avoid an unpleasant duty is to question its validity, and in his confusion Arjuna questions Krishna's insistence that he fight. Krishna explains that acting for a just cause is a worthy sacrifice and that inaction denies the active nature of the soul. He outlines sacrifice as part of a divine relationship between humans and nature which was set in motion at the dawn of time, and which was meant to "bestow upon you everything desirable." This divine plan encourages people to work according to their particular skills and to offer the results of their efforts to the Supreme Person—in essence, sanctifying all endeavors as acts of love. He also reveals more of his identity as that original Supreme Person and continues to nurture Arjuna's self-confidence by describing the nobility of the soul.

3.1–2 Arjuna said, "I am confused. Why would you have me fight this ghastly war if intelligence is better than selfish action?"

3.3–5 Krishna said, "There is no escaping karma merely by abstaining from action. Nor can you achieve success by giving up action. Further, all beings are obliged to act according to their *gunas*, or behavioral traits. No one can remain inactive even for a moment.

3.6–9 "You delude yourself by withdrawing externally from the world of the senses while internally remaining enamored of it.[40] You cannot even maintain your body without acting. Better than withdrawing is to engage your senses for a righteous purpose and dedicate whatever you do as an offering of love to the Supreme Person.

3.10–16 "Since the dawn of time, this has been the way of a holy life. The Supreme Being intended humanity to live comfortably by honoring the *devas*,[41] and the devas being pleased would supply life's necessities. 'Be prosperous by offering *yajna*[42] to the gods,' he said, 'for this will bestow upon you everything desirable.' Such cooperation with nature and her caretakers is sacred, and life without that sacred dimension is lived in vain.[43]

---

[40] Behind a yogi's serene façade may lurk copious dreams of sensual delight. As they say in French, *les robes ne font pas le moine* ("the robes don't make the monk").

[41] See "Topics in the Gita."

[42] The original meaning of *yajna* was formal fire ceremonies and animal sacrifices as prescribed in the Vedas. In the sense of "making sacred," anything we do can be a yajna if conducted with some formality and as a gesture of devotion.

[43] In a text filled with practical and contemporary insights into human nature, how do we accommodate references to fire ceremonies and sacrifices to the gods? Are they relics of earlier, less evolved times? Are they metaphorical? However we interpret the role of higher beings as depicted in the Gita's cosmology, these verses point to an imperative in devotional practice to recognize creation itself as a living being. Nature has as much sanctity as any other form of life, and there is

3.17–21 "Those who honor that divine plan have no other obligations. Great kings have always known this.[44] Like them, perform your duty for the good of the world; for people emulate the behavior of great souls.

3.22–25 "I am the Supreme Person. There is no work prescribed for me, yet I also honor prescribed duty. If I failed to perform my duties with care, others would follow that example to no good end. The wise are active, but they work without attachment just to set an example for others.[45]

---

an ominous note to the word *mogham*, "useless" or "in vain," which hints at dire consequences if we betray our responsibility to honor the earth's natural ecology.

[44] Good governance, in the Gita's worldview, combines *kshatriya* or protective skill (18.43), with respect for life's higher purpose. Apart from providing citizens with security and basic needs, the ancient Indian monarchs and kings referred to here encouraged the citizenry to follow the path of dharma. Indirectly, Krishna is putting down the Kauravas for failing in these dimensions of royal duty.

[45] At a conference in the 1970s, someone asked the late Gita scholar J.A.B. van Buitenen to summarize the Gita's position on work. "My understanding," he said, "is that Krishna tells Arjuna, 'I'm God, I don't need anything, I don't have anything to gain, and yet I'm working all the time. Who the hell do you think you are?'" Krishna's point here is that refusing to fight would bring no good end—a pointed contradiction of Arjuna's arguments to the contrary.

3.26–29 "The learned know better than to discourage the less learned from acting. Rather, they offer encouragement, knowing people are confused and think themselves the sole determinant of their actions. Actions are carried out by the gunas, but this is not understood by those who do not know their true self.[46]

3.30–35 "Offer your work to me without considering personal gain. If you follow my advice faithfully and without envy, then you will be free from the bondage of action. Do not deny your warrior nature, for repression accomplishes nothing. Both repression and attachment are stumbling blocks. Better to fail doing what you must than succeed in a dharma not your own, for that way is dangerous."[47]

3.36 Arjuna said, "What compels people to such self-defeating behavior?"

3.37–41 Krishna said, "You work against your best interests when you let unbridled cravings control you. Cravings spring from *rajo-guna* and deteriorate into anger. Ev-

---

[46] The meaning is that no one can do anything independent of the workings of nature. Things get done only with the cooperation of energies completely outside our control, but conditioned souls—persons who think themselves independent in their actions—make the mistake of taking credit (or blame) for everything they do.

[47] Arjuna wants to leave the battlefield to become a peaceful yogi, but Krishna says here he doesn't think it would last very long.

eryone is conditioned by their cravings to some degree, as a fire is covered by smoke, a mirror by dust, or an embryo by the womb. Cravings sit in the senses, the mind, and the intelligence and burn like an uncontrolled fire which devours knowledge and self-awareness. Begin, Arjuna, by mastering your senses which can overshadow common sense.[48]

3.42–43 "Above the senses is the mind, above the mind is intelligence, and above intelligence is the soul. Knowing yourself to be superior to the lower selves, rise up and master your impulsive desires."[49]

---

[48] While the Gita recognizes that to be human means to feel and have urges or "cravings" (*kama*), these verses warn that it is dangerous to indulge in excessive kama. Unbridled desires pose a danger to ourselves and to others.

[49] In scriptural accounts and personal memoirs advanced bhakti yogis describe what it is like to be a *jivanmukta*, or a soul liberated while still living in a material body. They report still feeling the impulses of the senses, occasional agitations of the mind, and speculations of the intellect; but these sensations do not distract their attention from the Supreme. The example is given of a coconut without milk: the meaty insides have dried and become detached from the shell. The consciousness of a jivanmukta is analogously "dried" of its material interests. Impulses come and go while the jivanmukta remains calm and steady, with consciousness fixed on the Supreme Person.

4

rishna describes the Gita's teachings as eternal and urges Arjuna to see them as an impetus to reconsidering his withdrawal from battle. He also gives further information about himself as the Supreme Person and advises Arjuna to learn the truths of life by serving a qualified guru. Since Krishna is serving in person as Arjuna's guru, the advice is offered on general principles: no one reaches enlightenment without the help of a teacher. In the last verse, Krishna exhorts Arjuna to use cumulative knowledge of the self, the Supreme Self, and the relationship of love that unites them as inspiration for cutting through his doubts and embracing the battle to come.*

4.1–3 Krishna said, "What I teach you is not new. At the dawn of the creation I taught this science of the self to the Sun God,[50] and it was passed down in a *parampara* succession of teachers. Over time, the teachings were lost.[51] I make you the new keeper of this wisdom because you are my friend and can understand its mysteries."

---

[50] Vedic cosmology, which views all natural phenomena as governed by highly evolved beings, ascribes a *deva* (demigod) to each planet and cosmic function. The Sun God in our universe is named Vivasvan.

[51] There have been many creations according to the Gita and there will be many others (8.17–19), and in each creation the Su-

4.4 Arjuna said, "Your birth came later. How is it possible that you taught this to the Sun God?"

4.5–9 Krishna said, "You and I are both eternal, Arjuna. Because my body is not different from me I remember the past, but you do not.[52] In each millennium when dharma is in decline, I appear in this world to protect the sadhus, subdue evildoers, and reestablish the path of righteousness. Those who understand this truth about my appearance and activities never return to the world of birth and death.[53]

4.10–15 "However people understand me, and however they offer themselves to me, I return their dedication in

———————————⬡———————————

preme Person reveals the Gita's teachings in one form or another. This passage suggests that over the millennia since Krishna first delivered his wisdom teachings to humanity on our particular planet, the true purpose of yoga was improperly interpreted and then lost altogether. Even today, yoga instruction often lacks the philosophical foundation that supports its ultimate purpose: the reawakening of love for the Supreme Person.

[52] Krishna's body is *sac-chit-ananda*: "eternal knowledge and bliss." Unlike conditioned souls born into material bodies, which are temporary outer casings, Krishna has a body of pure spirit. There is no difference between his physical form and himself. We finite souls, on the other hand, forget our previous lives because memories (with occasional exceptions) die with the body.

[53] There have been many *avatars* or "descents" of the Supreme Person. Because seven principal avatars appeared prior to Krishna's appearance, scholars often described him as the eighth incarnation of Vishnu. Still, the bhakti texts also describe Krishna as *avatari*, the source of all avatars (see Schweig 2005, pp.108–

kind. Most worship God for some end, according to their station in life. Those stations, called *varnas*,[54] were created by me. I am unchangeable and not subject to material designations. Nor is there any work that I am obligated to perform. In the past, many great souls have known this truth concerning my nature, and they acted with this understanding. Perform your duty, following their example.

4.16–23 "I will explain the meaning of karma, which challenges even brilliant minds. There is inaction, improper action, and proper action. Inaction, like improper action, carries karmic consequences.[55] To avoid karmic reaction, act without personal motive. There is no consequence to selfless work, which is work conducted without coveting its results. Those who are content with little, who envy no one, and are unshaken by either success

———————————————— ⬢ ————————————————

110). The inner significance of these many divine appearances is that the Supreme Person is concerned about his family: the many souls who suffer under the illusion of conditioned life. He comes again and again to call them back to him.

[54] This verse refers to the *varnashrama* system, which assigns people to social and vocational classes according to their skills and behavioral dispositions. These divisions are often referred to as the "caste system," although the original idea had nothing to do with repressing "lower castes" as has occurred in India over the past many centuries.

[55] "Action in inaction" in verse 18 refers to the consequences of apathy. If a child wanders into traffic, onlookers who stand idly by and do nothing are implicated in karmic reaction by their failure to come to the child's aid.

or failure—such souls are already free of all karmic consequences.

4.24–33 "Anything done by such holy people benefits the world. These yogis are inspired by different practices. Some worship devas with offerings into a sacrificial fire. Others control their sensual activity by various physical disciplines. Some follow the eightfold yoga path, some seek *jnana*[56] by studying sacred texts, and still others perform *prana*[57] exercises to control their breathing. All yoga is a preparation for liberation from the world of birth and death, all require some sacrifice, and all lead to knowledge of the Supreme Being.

4.34–35 "Acquire this knowledge by approaching a *guru*, or spiritual teacher, with humility, service, and questions. Having seen the truth, a realized soul can enlighten you.[58] Knowing that truth you will never again

---

[56] See "Topics in the Gita."

[57] *Prana* refers to breath or vital energy, comparable to the Chinese notion of Qi, which circulates throughout the body and can be stimulated through appropriate exercises.

[58] The words *tattva-darshinah* in verse 34 translate as "one who has seen the truth," i.e. a teacher with practical wisdom as well scholarship. There are many kinds of gurus, but the kind Krishna references here are spiritual masters who can lead students to achieve more than they think themselves spiritually capable: namely full self-realization. Some people assume that a guru will relieve them of having to make hard decisions by telling them what to do. My contact with spiritual teachers over the years has convinced me that the most gifted teachers

fall into illusion and will learn to see all beings as parts of me.

4.36–40 "Even if you commit the most grave offense, the boat of wisdom will carry you across the ocean of material miseries. How sublime is this knowledge, which burns to ashes all karmic consequences![59] Nothing can compare, for with this knowledge sincere seekers will know their true self in due course and attain eternal peace. Without such knowledge, life remains filled with doubt and faithlessness; and for the doubting soul there is happiness neither in this world nor the next.

4.41–42 "Immerse yourself in authentic yoga practice and get clear of doubts. Slash them with the weapon of knowledge.[60] Arm yourself with yoga, Arjuna, and then stand and fight."

———————————————— ◉ ————————————————

inspire students in such a way that they are able to make sense of scriptural teachings and apply them in their lives on their own. At the end of the Gita, for instance, Krishna tells Arjuna, "Reflect, and then do what you think best" (18.63).

[59] What kind of worldview do we find here? Krishna outlines a theology in which forgiveness and rectification triumph over past mistakes. There are no souls burning in hell or wrathful divinities. Instead, we find encouragement and acceptance that in the material world no one has a pretty story to tell and everyone deserves a second chance. To borrow a contemporary aphorism from Sikh saint Kirpal Singh (1894-1974), "Every sinner has a future, every saint a past."

[60] *Chittva*, to cut or slash, may seem like harsh language; but in effective yoga instruction a teacher must sometimes use straight talk to jolt a student out of harmful habits.

rjuna insists on further clarification from Krishna. How can Krishna expect him to fight yet not become implicated in the consequences of fighting? Krishna answers that even the actions of a soldier in battle, if undertaken with compassion and "for the good of all,"[61] can constitute dharma. Krishna again emphasizes his identity as the Supreme Person and assures Arjuna that the path to peace lies not in renouncing a difficult challenge but in remembering him within the heart and acting with devotion. The message is clear: Bhakti-yogis, those who serve others with love, live happily in this world. How do we gain sufficient distance from our own woes to put the well-being of others before our own? The Gita advises that we not judge the trials we face superficially: an eternal reality dwells beneath external appearances.

5.1 Arjuna said, "You urge me to avoid karma, but then encourage me to fight. Tell me, which of these is better?"

5.2–10 Krishna said, "Both renunciation (*sannyasa*) and work in devotion (*karma-yoga*)[62] are good. Still, work in

---

[61] The word *loka-sangraha*, "the good of all," appears only twice in the Gita, but many other verses underscore how dear those persons are to Krishna who put the well-being of others before their own.

devotion is better. It is childish to say that renouncing the world is superior to devotional yoga; merely renouncing activity cannot make anyone happy. Those who see the Self[63] in all beings and work for the good of all are never sullied by work, as a lotus flower is never sullied by swamp water.[64]

5.11–18 "A yogi who sanctifies the actions of body, mind, intelligence and senses by giving up the fruits of work lives happily even while in the city of nine gates,[65] knowing that neither the soul nor the Supreme Soul is responsible for the consequences of work. Knowledge of the soul's inviolable nature is like sunshine which destroys darkness. In that glorious light, misgivings disappear and the wise see with equal vision all beings:

---

[62] The difference between karma and *karma-yoga* is the difference between acting for oneself and acting as a gesture of devotion. See *karma* in "Topics in the Gita."

[63] Self refers here to both the individual self *(jiva-atma)* and also the Supreme Self *(paramatma)*. The dual meaning suggests that knowledge of our true self implies knowledge of the Supreme Self who dwells in our hearts.

[64] Lotus flowers grow in swamps yet swamp water does not adhere to the glossy surface of their leaves, an apt analogy for Krishna's point about karma not "sticking" to those who work in a selfless spirit. In brief, these verses declare that the devotional purpose of our actions has greater value than their technical content.

[65] The nine gates of the body are the eyes, nostrils, ears, mouth, anus, and genitals. To live happily in this city suggests a regulated diet, restraint in sensual indulgence, attention to habits of speech, and other yogic behavior.

a learned *brahmin*,[66] a cow, an elephant, a dog, and a dog eater.[67]

5.19–26 "In such equanimity, those who know their true self have already overcome the cause of repeated birth and death and enjoy inner contentment at every moment. They are undisturbed by duality, their sensual life is subdued, and they live in peace. Such yogis benefit the world and live in brahman.

5.27–29 "Those who know their true self are in full control of physical and mental functions. They remain free from unbridled desire, fear and anger and are liberated. Knowing that I pervade creation to accept their expressions of love, these yogis attain peace[68] from the pangs of material existence."

---

[66] The juxtaposing of *brahmin*, a member of the priest class, and dog eater is significant since brahmins are traditionally vegetarian. To see these two extremes "with equal vision" would indeed signify that misgivings, particularly concerning class distinctions, have dissapeared in the "glorious light" of seeing the soul within all bodies.

[67] While a bit of a stretch, some commentators interpret these verses as supportive of vegetarianism. For an analysis of vegetarianism as part of spiritual practice, see Steven Rosen, *Diet for Transcendence: Vegetarianism and the World Religions* (Badger, CA: Torchlight Publishing, 1997).

[68] See *rasas* in "Topics in the Gita" for an explanation of *shanti* (peace) as a preliminary stage of self-realization. The yogis described here have not yet reached the highest stage of yoga, which is identified in the final verse of the next chapter.

6

rishna has urged Arjuna to not leave the battlefield but to serve a greater good by fulfilling his duty in a spirit of bhakti, or devotional yoga. Now he reinforces that position with a disconcerting portrait of the austere yoga practiced by ascetics. Arjuna admits his inability to follow such an intense discipline and is worried: What will be my fate, he asks, if I fight yet cannot also reach perfection in yoga? Krishna assures him that progress in yoga is a permanent asset, which carries over from one life to the next. Whatever he is able to do by acting in a spirit of devotion will never be lost. "In all circumstances," Krishna says, "be a yogi." And in the final verse he concludes with an unequivocal statement on what constitutes the highest yoga.

6.1–7 "Those yogis who embrace their dharma without egoistic motive are the real *sannyasis*, Arjuna, not those who withdraw and do nothing. Yoga begins with postures and rises to uninterrupted mental equanimity, for the mind is either friend or foe. With mind controlled, the yogis commune with the Supreme Person in their heart and are inured to external conditions.

6.8–10 "Those who have achieved mental discipline regard everything—stones and gold, friends and foes—equally.[69] They are not motivated by personal ambition and keep to themselves in a peaceful frame of mind.

6.11–18 "If you still wish to practice yoga in seclusion, you must completely withdraw from the world. Cover kusha grass with deerskin[70] and a soft cloth. Devoid of sexual thoughts,[71] focus your mind on a single point, with body, head and neck aligned. Meditate upon me in your heart. Discipline your mind. Moderate your eating and sleeping, for there is no yoga without moderation.[72] Thus you will enter into the supreme *nirvana*.[73]

---

[69] The word *sama*, equitably disposed to all, does not mean that advanced yogis excuse criminal behavior or abstain from addressing wrongs but that they respond to wrongdoing with compassion rather than vengeance.

[70] Like a sword, the edges of the long-stemmed kusha grass are sharp (*kusha*) and thus symbolic of discernment or discriminating wisdom. A deerskin protects the meditator from getting cut by the sharp grass, but only skin of a deer that dies a natural death can be used for meditation. Killing a deer for its skin violates the principle of ahimsa.

[71] The Sanskrit phrase *brahmachari-vrata* means vow of celibacy. Sex is such a powerful impulse that it can impede yoga practice, which explains why traditional yoga schools encourage celibacy at least during the student years. The Gita also defines celibacy as faithfulness to one's life partner (7.11), but here Krishna admonishes Arjuna that if he is serious about advancing in yoga he must practice in a secluded place and abstain from sex altogether.

[72] There is, to my reading, some sarcasm here in Krishna's description of yoga practice: "You want to leave the battle-field and practice yoga? Okay, here is what you have to do. Get some kusa grass and go to a completely isolated location.

6.19–23 "As a lamp's flame in a windless place is perfectly still, so is the mind absorbed in yoga. In that stage called samadhi you will see your true self within yourself and know happiness so great that no greater happiness can be found. At that moment, even surrounded by extreme difficulties you will be unshakeable.

6.24–33 "Absorb yourself in this yoga and think of nothing else. If your mind wanders, pull it back. The yogis whose minds are fixed on me reach ultimate joy, knowing their qualitative oneness with me. True yogis, in love with me as I am with them, see me the Supersoul[74] in all beings, everywhere.[75] I am never lost to such souls, nor are they ever lost to me. By comparison with their own

———————————————————⊙———————————————————

Sit straight, discipline your mind, moderate your eating and sleeping..." Then he admonishes Arjuna that a real yogi does not leave the battlefield to practice yoga; real yogis live their yoga, seeing the Supreme Being everywhere.

[73] The popular understanding of *nirvana* is "cessation of existence"—basically, not having to deal with your family any more. "I'm gone. Leave me alone." A slightly more informed definition would be "beyond flickering," i.e. a place beyond material disturbances, like a candle in a windless spot. Buddhism describes nirvana as deathlessness, which is achieved by following the Noble Eightfold Path of virtuous behavior. As in this verse, the Gita emphasizes a different dimension of nirvana: namely a state of complete absorption in love for the Supreme Being.

[74] Readers will find details regarding *paramatma* (Supersoul), the Supreme Person situated in the heart of all beings, in footnotes to 10.10-11 and 13.13-19.

self these great yogis understand the true equality of all beings in their happiness and distress."[76]

6.34 Arjuna said, "The yoga practice you recommend strikes me as impossible. It is more difficult to control the mind than to control the wind."

6.35–36 Krishna said, "It can be done, through practice and discipline.[77] Strive to control the mind and your success is assured."

◈

---

[75] Terms such as "environment" and "globalization" had not been coined at the time of the Gita, yet these verses suggest that we are interconnected by the underlying divinity of all creation. When we learn to see that presence of the Supreme Being everywhere, in every molecule and creature on earth, we will have taken a step toward true civilization. Environmentalist Paul Hawken does a lovely job of explaining how interconnectedness translates into social action.

[76] Taken together, verses 24–33 form a concise roadmap to becoming a *parama-yogi* or "greatest yogi." The journey begins by engaging in yoga with determination and faith. The first objective is mental discipline, which is achieved through understanding the fact that we are qualitatively one with the Supreme Being. This leads to a happy demeanor ("I am protected, I have inner resources to draw on"), which in turn nurtures compassion ("All beings are also of the same spiritual nature as me"). A key phrase in this sequence is "by comparison with their own self," a succinct definition of empathy and a moving portrait of perfect yoga achieved by seeing paramatma in the hearts of all.

6.37–39 Arjuna said, "If I cannot—if I fail—what will be my fate? What is the fate of those who take to yoga but then fall away? Are they not lost between worlds, like a cloud with no place to call home?"

6.40–44 Krishna said, "Never fear. Even imperfect yogis cannot be touched by misfortune. If you die with your practice incomplete, you will first enjoy the fruits of your good work in a heavenly realm. After this you will be born into a righteous or well-to-do family,[78] or into a family of yogis—someplace favorable for resuming your journey to the pure self.[79] From there, by virtue of your previous practice, you will resume where you left off.

---

[77] The Gita describes discipline as necessary for developing a well-integrated, dynamic self-identity. Without discipline (through various contemplative practices and dietary and lifestyle regulation) *karma-yoga* deteriorates into rash actions, *jnana-yoga* into dry abstractions, and *bhakti-yoga* into sentiment and ritual.

[78] In theory, birth in a well-to-do family means not having to worry about the rent and having more free time for yoga and self-realization. In practice, given current market conditions, it doesn't always work out that way.

[79] To appreciate the value of a "righteous" family, we only need to look at the many dysfunctional, unrighteous families around us. Too few young people enjoy the blessing of a home where they are cared for and encouraged to nourish their soul, where yoga practice is understood and honored, and where they can learn to love and be loved. The promise here is that whatever spiritual progress we make in this life will not be lost. We pick up next time from wherever we stopped previously.

6.45–46 "With sincere practice you will then make further progress, dissipate any remaining karma, and come to me. Because yogis have a greater chance for success than ascetics, *jnanis*, and others, in all conditions, Arjuna, be a yogi.

6.47 "And of all yogis, those who love me as I love them are the greatest of all."[80]

---

[80] "To serve and get closer to God is the only reason to practice or to teach yoga," write Sharon Gannon and David Life, founders of Jivamukti Yoga. "Without the desire for God, *asana* (the physical dimension of yoga) is meaningless exercise. Without devotion, Yoga cannot be attained." (*Jivamukti Yoga: Practices for Liberating Body and Soul*, New York: Ballentine Books, 2002, p. 231)

 oing deeper into an explanation of his identity, Krishna says he is the source of all animate and inanimate energies and that no truth is superior to him. He describes four types of people who do not seek him and four types of people who do. Sincere souls who understand his identity give themselves to him in love and by virtue of that eternal bond are unaffected by illusion or death. In this chapter he also provides a sampling of ways to see him in creation, an exercise that he will conduct with greater detail in Chapter 10.

7.1–3 Krishna said, "Now hear, Arjuna, how you can know me in full by practicing yoga. I shall reveal to you knowledge both abstract and applied, knowing which you shall need to know nothing else.[81] Rare is the soul who seeks perfection and rarer still the soul who knows me in truth.

7.4–5 "Earth, water, fire, air, space, mind, intelligence, ego—these are my *prakriti*, or material energies. Beyond

---

[81] Enlightenment is sometimes mistaken as omniscience. "You shall need to know nothing else" means that once Arjuna masters the teachings of the Gita he will possess sufficient knowledge for acting in the world with devotion.

them is the life force, which includes the living beings who inhabit this material world.[82]

7.6–7 "Both matter and spirit come from me, and there is no truth higher than me. Everything rests on me as pearls strung on a thread.[83]

7.8–14 "I am the taste in water, the radiance of the moon and sun, the syllable AUM, the sound in ether, ability in all beings, the original fragrance of the earth, the heat in fire, the seed of all life, the intelligence of the wise, the prowess of the powerful. I am sexuality that honors dharma—and yet I remain apart from my creation. People deluded by their material conditioning do not know me. Only those who have given themselves to me remain impervious to the influence of my *maya*.

7.15 "Four kinds of souls do not offer themselves to me: those who are bewildered, those who have lost their hu-

---

[82] Living beings are called *tatastha-shakti*, or "marginal energy" (i.e. they live on the border between the material and spiritual energies). This marginal nature means they are susceptible to influence by *maya*, or forgetfulness.

[83] In these key verses, Krishna presents himself as the foundation of everything. He takes the rest of this chapter to provide supporting evidence of his supremacy. Yet soon after (9.26) he will admit that something can defeat him: a simple flower offered with love. The magnificence of bhakti lies in its superiority over majesty. Love for God, the Gita confirms, is the most powerful force in creation, for God himself is humbled by a simple sincere offering of love.

man qualities, those who are defiant, and those who are atheists.[84]

7.16–19 "Four kinds of people do offer themselves to me: the distressed, the curious, the impoverished, and the seekers of knowledge.[85] All are dear to me, but the seekers who know me and love me are dearest and most like my own self. It has taken them many births to reach enlightenment, and I am everything to them. Such souls are rare.[86]

7.20–25 "Most people worship lesser gods, and their satisfaction is meager. However people offer themselves to me I reciprocate, but the fruits of worship devoid of love are ephemeral. Those worshipers mistakenly think that I

---

[84] *Mudhah* translates as "bewildered beings" or more accurately "beasts of burden," i.e., people so preoccupied by responsibilities that they allow no time for contemplative practice. *Naradhamah* translates as "devoid of human qualities," indicating people whose self-destructive habits impede their ability to consider a life of devotion. *Mayayapahrita-jnanah* translates as "defiant," intellectuals whose intellect is itself the impediment to their devotion, i.e. a conceit which leaves no room for a personal Supreme Being. *Asuram bhavam asritah* translates as "atheists," those who take an active stance against the notion of a sentient agency behind creation.

[85] The people identified here are not realized yogis, although Krishna does characterize them as *sukritinah,* or "persons of character," inasmuch as they recognize Krishna's divinity. These verses describe that initially people may take to a path of self-realization motivated by some material need. With time, in the company of advanced souls and with daily yoga

was formless and that I assumed this personality to come into the world. Because my true identity is hidden from them by *yoga-maya*,[87] they do not know my imperishable higher nature as a person, unborn and inexhaustible.

7.26–29 "I know them, Arjuna, those who have passed on, those who live now, those yet to come. Me, no one knows, for all beings at the time of their birth emerge bewildered; all except those whose past lives have been virtuous and who live in virtue now. Such souls love me intensely and know themselves in truth.

7.30 "They understand brahman, they know that I am the very principle of the self, that I direct the material energy, that I live in their hearts, and they remain in yoga even at the time of death."

---

practice, they begin to shed material motives and develop real devotion.

[86] The phrase *vasudevah sarvam iti* in 7.19 is often translated: "Vasudeva (Krishna, son of Vasudeva) is everything." And technically, this is accurate since Krishna describes himself as the source of all temporary and eternal energies. If, however, we understand Krishna's purpose in the Gita as the reawakening of love for him, then this same phrase can be translated with a slight but significant nuance: "I am everything to them." For lovers, the beloved is everything. The great Vaishnava commentator Ramanuja (1017–1137) makes this point in his interpretation of the Gita (see Arvind Sharma, *The Hindu Gita: Ancient and Classical Interpretations of the Bhagavadgita*, La Salle, IL: Open Court, 1996, p. 119).

[87] See "Topics in the Gita."

rishna's instructions have calmed Arjuna and now he responds to Krishna's description of enlightenment by asking a series of penetrating questions. He wants to rise to the occasion and embrace his dharma but is still concerned about his fate should he die in battle. Krishna encourages him, saying that bhakti yogis do not take birth again in the material world but return to the eternal atmosphere to which all souls belong. Indeed, he says, those souls who dedicate their life to devotion already live in eternity even within their material bodies.

8.1–2 Arjuna said, "What is brahman? What is the principle of self? What is karma? And how can I know you at death?"

8.3–5 Krishna said, "Brahman refers to the indestructible soul. The principle of self refers to your eternal nature. Karma refers to actions you perform which produce material bodies.[88] By remembering me at the moment of death you will come to me. Of this there is no doubt.

---

[88] Good and bad actions both generate material bodies. Acting with the best of intentions may be preferable to acting in a hurtful manner, but the performer is still obliged to come back in a material body to reap the benefits of such charitable deeds.

8.6–9 "Indeed, whatever souls remember at death determines their destination.[89] So think of me, Arjuna, and fight. Do not allow your mind to deviate from your duty even for a moment. Remember me as the knower of everything, the primordial being, within every atom, whose inconceivable transcendental form is luminous like the sun.

8.10–11 "At the moment their soul leaves the body, those who are absorbed in bhakti yoga come to me. Let me describe what awaits you after death, a place coveted by austere sages, and how it is attained.

8.12–16 "The physical yoga practice seeks to withdraw all thought from external objects. It fixes the mind on the heart and elevates the life air to the top of the head. If, at the moment of quitting the body, the yogi vibrates the sacred syllable AUM and remembers me, such a person goes to the supreme destination. Once having come to me, these accomplished yogis never return to this temporary and problematic world.

8.17–19 "Brahma, the first being in the universe, appears at the dawn of time, and all others souls appear in this world after him. A thousand ages pass, and life is again absorbed into the non-manifest brahman[90] in a perpetual cycle of creation and destruction.

---

[89] The Gita teaches that thoughts, hopes, desires—the "subtle" body of this life—determine the "gross" body of our next life. The physical form we now inhabit is the product of our state of mind at the moment we left our previous lifetime.

[90] This cycle of cosmic creation and destruction is detailed in two classic Sanskrit texts, among others: the Bhagavata

8.20–22 "But another place exists, which is eternal and indestructible. When this world ends that other one remains and once going there no one returns to this material world. I am there but I am here, too, with those who love me.

8.23–26 "Those who practice mystic yoga concern themselves with passing away at just the right moment, during the auspicious fortnight of the waxing moon or while the sun travels north. Those who die in light achieve brahman. Those who die in darkness return to the world of birth and death.[91]

8.27–28 "Such considerations mean nothing to the truly accomplished yogis. Their love surpasses scriptural mechanisms and all considerations of when and when not to die. They have already achieved eternity."

Purana and the Brahma Samhita. Krishna's point is that the material world may seem like a permanent reality since it lasts such a long time; yet, ultimately, it too dies. The only lasting reality is the soul and its relationship with him in the eternal world to which he alludes in verse 20 of this chapter.

[91] Prolonged practice of mystic eightfold (*astanga*) yoga stimulates extraordinary energies in the body. Advanced yogis master life airs on which their soul floats and gradually raise the soul through *chakras* or energy centers, until it reaches the cranial opening (*brahma-randhra*). They maintain themselves poised at that crucial exit point until they come to an astrologically favorable moment for leaving the body. The soul then bursts through the cranial opening and journeys to its intended destination. The Gita dismisses these exercises in the next verses as a kind of mystical tourism, since even advanced yogis must return to earth if they fail to achieve devotion.

9

cholarship may narrowly define the Gita as a historic document coming out of India, but it is also a timeless guide for humanity's journey to enlightenment. Here Krishna goes to the heart of human experience by differentiating between religion and love. He describes love as the nature of all souls, an emotion prompted by the mystery of creation and expressed in joyous song (kirtan), in devotional offerings of water and flowers, and in celebration of the relationship that unites all souls. The chapter also includes additional details concerning Krishna's personhood and the equality of all beings regardless of their material status—the equivalent of a millennia-old declaration of human rights.

9.1–3 "Because you are not envious of me I now give you even more intimate wisdom,[92] which will free you from misfortune. Here is the summit of knowledge, the most secret of all secrets[93] and the highest expression of grace. Because it leads to direct perception of the Self it is the

———————————————⟡———————————————

[92] Two words occur in the first verse: *jnana* (knowledge) and *vijnana*, (realized knowledge or wisdom). Jnana is theoretical while vijnana is applied. See *jnana* in "Topics in the Gita."

[93] The Gita is a secret among secrets not because it is hidden— Krishna tells Arjuna plainly (18.68–69) that those who spread the message of the Gita are most dear to him—but rather be-

perfection of dharma, everlasting, and joyfully applied. Those who lack faith in this dharma will not understand this, for theirs is the path of repeated birth and death.

9.4–10 "By my impersonal energies I pervade creation. All beings are in me yet I remain apart, my own person. Creation and all life emanate from me and are absorbed back into me at the end of each cosmic cycle, yet I remain neutral. The material energy by which the universe is continually created and destroyed operates under my direction.

9.11–12 "Those who do not understand my true nature think my body is something I assumed for coming into the world. Bereft of higher knowledge, they turn to philosophies which lead to confusion and hopelessness.[94]

---

cause nobody is interested. "Rare is the soul who seeks perfection," he says in 7.3, "and rarer still the soul who knows me in truth."

[94] Arriving in India in the 1700s, the British initially maintained a neutral attitude toward Hindu beliefs: they were there for trade, not cultural conquest. By the 1830s, however, missionaries had arrived and were shocked by the intimacy of Krishna worship. A god who engaged in relationships with women and who was worshiped as an "idol" in temples epitomized everything they found distasteful about India. If ever the "Hindoo heathens" were to become truly civilized (Europeanized) they would have to abandon such crude practices. The missionaries were not completely wrong in their dismissal of Krishna worship. Since the seventeenth century, the bhakti community had been sullied by cultists who disguised unrestrained sexual acts, among other spurious practices, as devotion to Krishna. Missionaries

⋑ LEFT: *"That Krishna himself was a historical figure is indeed quite indubitable."* —*Rudolph Otto (1869–1939), in* The Original Gita. ⋐

9.13–14 "Great souls who are not deluded know my true nature and I shelter them. They worship me, they constantly chant my name[95] with joy, and they offer me their love.

9.15–19 "Others worship God as one without a second or as Mother Nature, but it is I who am the Father of creation, the origin of scripture, the foundation of all that is, the refuge and dear-most friend, the source of heat and rain, of life and death.

---

were, in effect, reacting not to true bhakti culture but to deviant misrepresentations. Krishna as depicted in the Gita, on the other hand, conformed well to their sensibilities. Here was a hero, a wise teacher, espousing restraint and good character. This Krishna could legitimately serve as role model for a nation seeking acceptance on the world stage, and the intimate Krishna of the Bhagavata Purana fell into disrepute. India's religious leaders had never been trained for an encounter with European Enlightenment and were ill-equipped to defend Krishna worship; and Hindu intellectuals, for their part, cared more about bringing India into modern times than justifying temple rituals. By the mid 1800s Hindu social reformers had begun sanitizing India's religious culture by denigrating the parts that Modernity found offensive—arguing, for instance, that worship of deities was the vestige of an earlier and less civilized period of India's history. Krishna, they claimed, was not the ultimate goal of Hinduism but merely the crude expression of a higher, impersonal truth. The resurrection of authentic bhakti practice began in the late nineteenth century with scholar-devotees such as Bhaktivinode Thakur and Bhaktisiddhanta Saraswati, his successor as head of the Gaudiya Vaishnava community. In the 1960s, Bhaktisiddhanta's distinguished disciple A.C. Bhaktivedanta Swami Prabhupada brought authentic bhakti tradition to the West.

9.20–22 "Religionists who study the Vedas acknowledge me externally, making offerings intended to earn them heavenly rewards. Once those rewards are exhausted, they return to this mortal world. But for those who have no other goal but me and who adore me fully through their yoga, I preserve what they have and provide what they need.[96]

9.23–25 "Faith that seeks worldly benefit is misplaced. While such faith may lead to heavenly rewards, only my loving devotees live with me.

9.26–28 "If one offers me with love a leaf, a flower, a fruit, or some water, I accept.[97] Whatever you do or eat

---

[95] *Kirtan,* or devotional chanting, although only mentioned this one time in the Gita, is a seminal bhakti practice. Elsewhere (10.25) Krishna also declares that he is personally present in the meditative repetition of his names (*japa*).

[96] Krishna's promise here underscores the deeply personal nature of the relationship he has with his devotees. He feels so indebted to those who approach him with love that there is nothing he will not do to encourage them. While aspiring devotees may still have to contend with past karmic reactions, Krishna promises that they will lack nothing required for their devotional life.

[97] A name for Krishna is *bhava-grahi,* meaning that he does not see the material worth of an offering; he sees the loving mood (*bhava*) with which it is offered. Verse 26 exposes the hypocrisy of caste brahminism by declaring that anyone can engage in devotional service, since offering a leaf or cup of water requires neither great wealth nor birth in a brahmin family.

or perform, do so with me in your heart and nothing will bind you to this world.[98]

9.29–31 "I am equal to all, but anyone who is my friend I am their friend. Even those who have committed a serious offense I consider to be sadhus because they have taken to the path of devotion with determination and seriousness of purpose.[99] A sincere soul regrets doing wrong and quickly returns to a righteous and peaceful life. My devotee is never lost.

9.32–34 "The supreme goal is denied to none, not to women, *vaishyas* or *shudras*, let alone priests and saintly kings. All were born into this ephemeral and unhappy world. Now think of me, offer me your love, absorb yourself in me and surely you will come to me."[100]

---

[98] There is a Zen saying, "Before enlightenment, chop wood and carry water. After enlightenment, chop wood and carry water." The Gita advocates the bhakti equivalent of this focused approach to life in which everything we do, however mundane, is done with devotional intent. Nothing could be more meaningful than this verse for those of us who live in a time when multitasking robs everything of meaning.

[99] In contrast to his uncompromising position toward the arrogant Kauravas, here Krishna advocates forgiveness for those who regret their offenses and show "determination and seriousness of purpose" in their devotion. The South African Truth and Reconciliation Commissions were predicated on a similar principle of forgiveness for those who expressed sincere remorse for wrongs of the past and worked to compensate for the harm they did.

⊰ LEFT: *"Beloved Krishna dwells in my heart," sings bhakti poet Mirabai (1498–1547).* ⊱

---

[100] My take on this verse is that it exposes stratification according to sex or race as an empty convention. Judging by his statements elsewhere, Krishna makes no such distinctions. His instruction here is a reprimand to elitists who deem women and people born into "lower castes" inferior or irrelevant.

10

t is remarkable how often Krishna reminds Arjuna that their discussion is predicated on friendship and love. Arjuna acknowledges that he has heard things about Krishna's divinity before but that it is only now, listening to Krishna's words with an open heart, that he begins to understand who Krishna is. Krishna responds with a poetic recitation of ways to see him in the world, essentially by identifying things which are superlative in every category of life. It is as if he is saying to those of us not yet able to see him in his original form, "Here I am, in ways you can perceive." The Supreme Being uses every means possible to help us remember him: He dwells in our hearts as paramatma, he steps out of our hearts to reveal himself through scriptures and teachers, and he appears around us every second of every day as the wonders of the universe.

10.1–2 "Arjuna, because you are my friend I will share with you knowledge of myself even deeper than what we have spoken so far. Even great demigods[101] do not know these dimensions of my being.

---

[101] Ancient India's cosmology describes *devas*, or demigods, such as Brahma, Shiva, Indra, Durga, and Ganesh as empowered beings charged with various departments of universal maintenance.

10.3–7 "Those who know me as unborn and unparalleled in all the worlds[102] are free from misfortune. They recognize me as the source of life's qualities such as happiness and distress, birth and death, fear and fearlessness, intelligence, forgiveness, truthfulness, self-control, freedom from doubt—all are created by me. All beings populating the many worlds[103] come from me. Those who know this are, without doubt, joined with me in yoga.

10.8–9 "I am the source of all material and spiritual worlds. Those who know this become immersed in feelings of love for me. They offer me their very life and constantly enliven one another by talking about me with joy. [104]

---

[102] Krishna has used this term *loka-maheshvaram* before (5.29). Its literal meaning is "supreme master of all worlds," a formal title which feels at odds with his devotional purpose in the Gita. Apart from its accuracy (as the source of creation he does qualify as "supreme master of all worlds"), he might be looking to differentiate himself from other deities. The culture at the time of the Gita acknowledged numerous demigods, many of them possessing their own worlds. The implicit statement here is "don't mistake me for one of them."

[103] The Sanskrit texts describe that life populates every planet of the universe, although not always in forms which are either familiar or visible to the naked eye.

[104] Keeping good company is the most critical element of effective bhakti practice. Among all yoga practices, bhakti is the most communal and includes discussion with others on the devotional path, friendship, and shared realizations. Without such good company, determination to maintain daily practice can wane.

10.10–11 "To such ecstatic souls who always endeavor to please me I offer *buddhi-yoga*,[105] the insight by which they can come to me. Dwelling in their hearts, I dispel the darkness of ignorance with the shining lamp of knowledge."[106]

10.12–15 Arjuna said, "You are the Supreme Brahman, the ultimate destination, eternal and transcendent. In the past, great teachers such as Narada and Vyasa have declared this about you and now you yourself confirm their statements.[107] I accept what you have told me, for without this revelation no one can know your true identity. You alone know who you are, O lord of all beings and master of the universe.

10.16–18 "Tell me in detail, O Supreme Yogi,[108] about your divine nature and the ways by which I can remember

---

[105] *Buddhi-yoga*, "the yoga of intelligence," is a technical term for yogic insight or the ability to intellectually filter all experience through the lens of our journey to self-realization.

[106] One of the Gita's fundamental teachings is that the Supreme Person literally dwells in our heart, not as poetic metaphor but as substantive reality. *Paramatma*, or Supersoul, is a full incarnation of the Supreme Person who accompanies the individual soul at every moment as friend and mentor. This four-armed form is the object of meditation in bhakti and mystic (*astanga*) yoga practices. Krishna in effect says there is a tangible, everpresent relationship binding him to all souls and that his investment in that relationship is complete to the extent of accompanying conditioned souls through their many lifetimes until they reach liberation. The *Mundaka-Upanishad* describes the soul and Supersoul as two birds in the same tree (material body). The conditioned soul bird attempts to enjoy the fruits of

you. I am never satiated hearing about you, for the more I hear the more I savor your sweet words."

10.19–21 Krishna said, "Yes, I shall tell you about my powers but only the most prominent, for there is no end to them. I am the Self dwelling in everyone's heart. I am the beginning, the middle, and the end of all beings. I am the light of the sun and moon and stars.

10.22–29 "Among the Vedas, I am *Sama*.[109] Among devas, I am their king. Among senses, I am the mind—and in all beings I am consciousness. I am Shiva, and the Lord of Wealth, Kuvera. I am the fire god Agni. Among mountains, I am Meru.[110] Of bodies of water, I am the ocean.

---

the tree. The Supersoul bird does not interfere but attempts as far as possible to offer advice and guidance.

[107] By referring to *rishayah sarve*, "all the great teachers," Arjuna avoids the misimpression that his acceptance of Krishna as the Supreme Brahman is mere flattery prompted by their friendship.

[108] By calling Krishna Supreme Yogi or Master of Yoga, Arjuna suggests not only that all yogic powers flow from him but also that he plays a critical role in our yoga progress. We do not make such progress on our own; advancement in yoga is bestowed upon us when, by our sincerity, we become worthy of it.

[109] India's earliest wisdom texts are the four Vedas, of which the *Sama-Veda* is considered to have been first. See *Vedas* in "Topics in the Gita."

[110] Sanskrit texts describe Meru as a golden mountain standing at the center of creation.

Of vibrations, I am the sacred AUM. I am *japa*, the chanting of holy names. Of immovable things, I am the Himalayas. Of trees, I am the banyan.[111] Among men, I am the monarch. Among weapons, I am the thunderbolt. Among cows, I am the wish-fulfilling *surabhi*.[112] I am both the impetus for creation and Yama, the Lord of Death.[113]

10.30–36 "Among beasts, I am the lion. Among birds, I am Garuda.[114] Of purifiers, I am the wind. Of weapon-bearers, I am King Rama.[115] Of fishes, I am the shark—of rivers, the Ganges. Of creators I am the beginning, the middle, and the end. Of knowledge, I am self-knowledge. Among logicians, I am conclusive truth. Of letters, I am 'A'.[116] I am

---

[111] The banyan tree, or Ashwattha, is one of India's tallest and most beautiful, often worshiped as part of daily ritual.

[112] The word *surabhi* literally means "sweet smelling." Devotional scriptures state that after liberation the soul returns to an eternal world where everything including trees and animals is endowed with mystic prowess. The cows in this magnificent realm not only give sweet-smelling milk but also fulfill the heart's every desire.

[113] All natural forces have personal representation in Gita cosmology. Death, too, is not without its guiding hand, although devotees generally prefer to meditate on Krishna as the supreme lovable object.

[114] Garuda is a giant eagle who provides transportation for Vishnu, the Supreme Being appearing in a four-armed form. Such interaction with nonhuman creatures is common in the bhakti texts, which describe a time long ago when humans, animals, and divine personalities such as Garuda frequently communicated.

inexhaustible time. Among creators, I am the many-faced Brahma. I am death, and the coming into being of all that is. Of feminine qualities, I am fame, splendor, eloquence, remembrance, perseverance and patience. Of prayers, I am *gayatri*.[117] Of seasons, I am flower-bearing spring. Of cheats, I am gambling.[118] I am the splendor of the splendid. I am victory, adventure, and the strength of the strong.

10.37–42 "And among the Pandavas, I am you, Arjuna. There is no end to my powers. What I have spoken is but a hint. All things glorious and excellent are but particles of my being. What need is there of such detail? A mere speck of my energies supports the universe itself."[119]

---

[115] There are two Ramas to whom this reference might apply, both of whom are honored by the bhakti tradition as avatars of Krishna. The first is Parasurama, renowned for his warrior prowess. The second is Rama, hero of Sage Valmiki's epic Ramayana and exemplar of ideal political leadership.

[116] "A" is both the first letter of the alphabet and the first sound in AUM.

[117] The *gayatri* mantra is one of the most important prayers in India's faith traditions. It is considered the incarnation of brahman and the essence of all four Vedas.

[118] Gambling may be the greatest cheat of all and so, as the superlative in its category, also represents Krishna.

[119] Krishna's poetic recitation of superlatives in this chapter is meant to reassure seekers of God that there is never a moment when we cannot find him around us. Everything is connected with the divine source of all creation, and with the proper vision even everyday objects and occurrences can be an inspiration to devotional practice.

*T*wo of the more difficult topics to grasp in the Gita are the personhood of Krishna, which is addressed throughout the dialogue, and Krishna's Cosmic or Universal Form, which is revealed in this chapter. If the notion of God as a unique individual challenges our sense of personhood, in Chapter 11 we confront enough horror to question whether God is truly all good. Here in one terrifying vision Krishna reveals for Arjuna the chaos that defines material life: destruction, disaster, suffering, the triumph of death over human endeavor—all life defeated by seemingly cruel and arbitrary powers. Faced with such apparent injustice, how does Arjuna react? At first he is understandably frightened and bewildered. Perhaps he expected a less shocking vision, given the poetic description Krishna just offered of himself in the last chapter: trees and mountains, sun and moon. Then, after the initial shock of seeing the Universal Form, Arjuna makes an astonishing gesture of his love for Krishna: he asks to be forgiven for underestimating him. "Sometimes I have been too casual with you," he says, "not adequately respectful. Can you forgive me, as a father would a son, as a friend would a friend, as a lover would a beloved?" Rather than blaming God for the ills of the world, Arjuna admits his inability to fathom God's purpose.

11.1–4 Arjuna said, "You have favored me with confidential knowledge, and it has erased my illusion. Still, I wish to see your Cosmic Form. If you think I am able to see it, please reveal to me that unlimited universal Self."[120]

11.5–8 Krishna said, "Behold those hundreds and thousands of forms, Arjuna, which no one has seen before. Behold in this one place the entire universe, all moving and non-moving beings, everything you have asked to see. Because you cannot witness this with your present eyes I give you divine eyes. Now, see my yoga powers!"

11.9–11 Sanjaya said, "O King Dhritarashtra, then Krishna, the master of all mystic yoga, revealed his Universal Form.[121] In that form Arjuna saw unlimited mouths and eyes, unlimited weapons, everything wondrous and expanding without end.

11.12–14 "If thousands of suns were to rise at once, their brilliance might resemble the effulgence of that universal form. Bewildered and astonished, Arjuna bowed his head and joined his palms in prayer."[122]

---

[120] Some bhakti commentators note that by this point in their talk Arjuna's doubts about Krishna have been resolved, and that asking to see his Universal or Cosmic Form is for the benefit of others who in the future may need further evidence of Krishna's divinity.

[121] The *Virata Rupa* or Universal Form is a manifestation of the Supreme Person which only appears within the material universe. Unlike Krishna's eternal humanlike form, which stimulates love, the Universal Form provokes awe, reverence, and fear.

[122] Joining palms is a universal gesture of respect for the divinity in the hearts of all beings.

11.15–23 Arjuna said, "I see all the divinities in your body, Brahma, Shiva and others. I see countless arms and bellies and eyes—there is no beginning or end to this. This form radiates a blinding light. I know now: You are the supreme object of all seeking. You are the eternal original person. Blazing fire shoots from your mouths and burns the universe. The three worlds[123] tremble at this sight, while celestial beings are amazed and cry out with prayers. Like them, I am afraid.

11.24–31 "I cannot bear to see these blazing faces and gaping mouths and fearsome teeth. Be merciful to me! I see the sons of Dhritarashtra and their armies and mine as well, all rushing into those flaming mouths. I see their heads crushed by those frightful teeth. They die likes moths in a fire. You lick the worlds with your horrible, scorching rays. Who are you? What is your mission? I do not understand."[124]

11.32–34 Krishna said, "I am time, destroyer of worlds.[125] Except for you, the soldiers assembled here will all be slain.

---

[123] Indian cosmology identifies three realms in the material universe: upper worlds, inhabited by *sattvic* or generous souls; middle worlds such as Earth, which shelter a wide variety of behaviors; and lower worlds, where awareness of life's higher purpose is all but extinguished. Earth is considered an ideal place for yoga practice: both heavenly and hellish conditions abound, providing dramatic points of reference and a powerful impetus for pursuing higher consciousness.

[124] Krishna makes no excuses for this side of his nature, although the Universal Form raises questions about the role of

Arjuna is terrified by the vision of Krishna's Universal Form.

evil and suffering. Why, for instance, does Arjuna see his own soldiers being crushed as mercilessly as the Kaurava soldiers? Only a few verses in the Gita are given over to suggesting why bad things happen to good people; most of the text concentrates on how we can extract ourselves from a world where no one can avoid bad things altogether. While Krishna has obliged Arjuna by showing him this frightening side of his nature, throughout the Gita he urges Arjuna (and through Arjuna, all souls) to see him not as the source of horror but as the source of love.

Therefore, get up, fight and reclaim your kingdom. They are already dead. Be the instrument of victory."

11.35 Sanjaya said, "Arjuna spoke with a faltering voice and head bowed."

11.36–40 Arjuna said, "The world rejoices, demons flee, the righteous bow down. Why should they not? You are the original creator, God of gods, the Cause of all causes. By you the universe is pervaded. I bow to you over and over, from all sides. You are everything.

11.41–42 "Out of affection or carelessness, I thought of you as my friend and rashly called you 'O Krishna, O my friend,' without knowing better. If I have disrespected you in any way, while we were playing or resting or eating together, I beg your forgiveness.

11.43–46 "No one is equal to you. Please excuse my offenses, as a father would those of a son, or a friend those of a friend, or a lover those of a beloved. I am gladdened by what I see but still I am afraid. Be gracious to me and show me again the form of yours which I knew before."

---

[125] Theoretical physicist Robert Oppenheimer (1904–1967) is remembered for his role as director of the Manhattan Project, which developed history's first nuclear weapons during World War II. When his team at Los Alamos National Laboratory in New Mexico tested their first atomic bomb, Oppenheimer (who was a student of the Gita) cited two verses from this chapter: "If the radiance of a thousand suns were to burst at once into the sky," he quoted, "that would be like the splendor of the Mighty One. Now I am Death, the destroyer of worlds."

11.47–49 Krishna said, "No one has seen what you have seen. This vision cannot be attained by study of scripture or sacrifice or great penance. You are disturbed by this frightening and awesome form. Do not be afraid. Be at peace and see again the form you long to see."

11.50 Sanjaya said, "Krishna then reverted to his own form as before, beautiful and tender, and Arjuna was pacified."

11.51 Arjuna said, "I am settled, seeing again your gentle humanlike form."

11.52–55 Krishna said, "This original personal form you see now is rarely seen even by exalted demigods. No one sees me as I am except by offering me love. One who is friendly to all and offers me love—that one comes to me, Arjuna."[126]

---

[126] A common feature in bhakti poetry and commentaries is a near indifference on the part of devotees to Krishna's identity as the Supreme Person. Advanced yogis reawaken their eternal *rasa* or relationship with Krishna through devotional practices and see him as their friend, child, or lover. They may sometimes think about his position as Supreme Being, but they do not hold it against him or let it interfere with their more intimate vision of him as the object of their love. Readers interested in studying the details of divine love might like to refer to Prabhupada's *Nectar of Devotion* (Los Angeles: Bhaktivedanta Book Trust, 1970).

12

rjuna's response to what he has just seen is unexpected. He seems to go off in a different direction, asking a philosophical question as though nothing had happened. Unless we look beneath the surface of his question it might appear that something is out of place, which has led some scholars to conclude the Universal Form was added at a later date. My meditations on the Gita have led me to a different conclusion. If we accept the Gita as a real discussion between real people, then the subtext of Arjuna's response makes sense. Is it better, he asks, to love you, knowing that you have this horrible side to your nature, or to admire you as an all-pervasive impersonal energy? And if we accept the Gita as a discussion between friends, then Krishna's reply also makes sense. I understand, he says, why you would prefer me without the dark role I sometimes play in human affairs; but denying my personhood will not resolve that. If you cannot have faith in me because of what you have seen, then perform a different yoga other than bhakti. Your faith in me may waver, but my faith in you will not and I will love you for whatever you can do.

12.1 Arjuna said, "Who has the better understanding of yoga, those who worship you in love or those who worship formless brahman?"

12.2–8 Krishna said, "Those who fix me in their mind and have faith in me are the highest yogis. Eventually, those who worship brahman—that which is beyond perception—also reach me, but their path is troublesome and their progress difficult.[127] For those who dedicate their lives to me in devotional yoga, I soon become their deliverer from the ocean of birth and death.[128] Fix me in your mind and we will live together, forever, without doubt.[129]

12.9–14 "If you are not able to fully absorb your mind in me, then develop devotion by practice of yoga. If you cannot, then devote your actions to me. This too will bring you to perfection. If you cannot do this either, then rely on me and act charitably in self-knowledge. Knowledge is

———————————————— ◈ ————————————————

[127] The Supreme Being has two features: *saguna* (a person endowed with form and qualities) and *nirguna* (formless, impersonal energy). The impersonal aspect found its most eloquent voice in Shankaracharya (788–820), founder of the school of Advaita Vedanta. Representatives of the personalist school include Ramanuja (1017–1137), Madhva (1238–1317), Nimbarka (usually ascribed to the thirteenth century although there is confusion over his dates), and Chaitanya (1486–1522). In the Gita, Krishna says that impersonal understanding of his nature is incomplete and that the fulfillment of love derives from knowing him as a person separate from his energies. See for example 6.47, 7.19, and 14.27.

[128] The words *na chirat*, "not after a long time" (i.e. soon), reminds us that enlightenment does not usually happen in a blinding flash. It takes time to overcome many births in the material world. Our conditioning runs deep and we should be patient if results do not happen instantly. Still, Krishna indicates here that of all yoga practices bhakti may be the swiftest.

[129] Just where they will live together is hinted at in 15.6.

better than practice, meditation is better than knowledge, and selfless action is better than meditation. One who is selfless, friendly and compassionate to all beings, steady in both happiness and distress, who is a self-controlled yogi and given over to loving service—such a soul is dear to me.

12.15–19 "One who never disturbs others and is never disturbed by others is dear to me. And one who is dear to me is free of anxiety and fear. One who is equal to all, who is composed under all conditions, who avoids bad company and is indifferent to praise and blame, who is moderate in speech, self-satisfied, and who shows me love—such a soul is dearly loved by me.

12.20 "But here is the essence of dharma: those who are my bhaktas, who have taken me into their hearts with faith, are the most dearly loved by me among all."[130]

---

[130] Describing those who keep him in their hearts as "most dear" is not sectarian. Krishna loves all beings, but it is natural to give extra attention to those whose reciprocation is full-hearted.

13

nce again, *Arjuna's response seems at odds with his situation on the battlefield. How should we understand his detour into questions of high philosophy—"What is knowledge, what is the object of knowledge"—and Krishna's willingness to go along with this line of inquiry, while vast armies stand poised around them ready to fight to the death? Might it be that they are absorbed in a miraculous inner world and have become oblivious to external circumstances? Such is the description of* samadhi, *or trance, given in sacred texts, including the Gita itself: "Happiness so great that no greater happiness can be found" and so complete that "even surrounded by the greatest difficulties you will be unshakeable" (6.19–23).*

13.1 Arjuna said, "I wish to learn about nature, about the field and the knower of the field, about knowledge and its object."

13.2–5 Krishna said, "The physical body is called 'the field,' and the eternal Self—the consciousness within the body—is called 'the knower of the field.' You should see me as the knower of all fields. Knowledge means understanding both field and knower. I will explain these subjects briefly, since they are already described by sages in numerous hymns and sacred texts.

13.6–7 "The field consists of five gross elements,[131] ego, intelligence, the gunas, ten senses,[132] mind, five sense objects,[133] desires and aversions, happiness and suffering, the assemblage of all these, plus the symptoms of life,[134] and the knower's convictions—these are the elements of the field and their interactions.

13.8–12 "Humility; forthrightness; nonviolence; patience; honesty; service to one's teacher; purity; self-control; equanimity; egolessness;[135] awareness of one's vulnerability to birth, death, old age, and disease;[136] a balanced concern for family duties; aversion to needless socializing; regard for self-awareness; devotion to me and to truth— these are called the constituents of knowledge.

---

[131] The five gross elements (*maha-bhuta*) are earth, water, fire, air, and sky.

[132] The ten senses include five senses for acquiring knowledge (eyes, ears, nose, tongue, skin) and five working senses (voice, legs, hands, anus, genitals).

[133] The five sense objects are smell, taste, form, touch, and sound.

[134] The symptoms of life are birth, growth, sustenance, procreation, deterioration, and death.

[135] Krishna has already mentioned humility as the first element of knowledge. His reference here to *an-ahankara* or "egolessness" means lack of material ego, i.e. the ability to act without selfish intent.

[136] The Gita advocates two visions of our mortality. Birth, for example, is described both as the mechanical consequence of karma and also an opportunity to do good and evolve as

13.13–19 "The knowledge needed for attaining immortality teaches that the Supreme Brahman pervades creation.[137] His hands, legs, eyes, and ears are everywhere. He transcends material definition, yet he dwells in all. As the Supersoul[138] he is the source of knowledge and light dwelling in everyone's heart and, though appearing divided among all beings, he remains one. Those who love me understand these truths and come to me.

13.20–22 "Regarding nature, both nature and life itself are eternal. Their apparent changes are products of the provisional material energy. Nature provides the tools, and with them living beings fashion their destiny. By that

---

yogis. Old age, disease, and death receive similar dual treatment, viewed in some verses as *kleshas* or material miseries and in others such as 13.8-12 as "constituents of knowledge." If life's hardships cause distress, these verses urge us to also see them as an impetus to spiritual practice.

[137] Krishna frequently refers to himself in the third person such as Supreme Brahman and Supersoul, a convention that may indicate his desire that Arjuna see him as a person separate from his functions in creation.

[138] By number of references alone, paramatma, or Supersoul, ranks among the Gita's most important topics. The idea that there is a voice of wisdom within us has more than poetic significance in the Gita, which describes a tangible presence of the Supreme Person dwelling in the heart of all beings. This soul-within-the-soul is the source of inspiration, a silent witness to our every thought, word, and deed. He provides guidance which can be perceived when the agitations of the mind are controlled through yoga practice.

contact with the gunas, they migrate through various species and vacillating conditions.

13.23–24 "Yet in the body, too, is the Supersoul, who sees and sanctions. Know this, and you will not take birth again.

13.25–30 "Some seek the Supersoul through meditation, others through study or selfless works. Some simply hear of him and are moved to worship. Such faith in proper instruction also leads to liberation from birth and death, for those who know that the Supersoul dwells within each living being and that neither the Supersoul nor the soul perishes—they truly see.

13.31–35 "Those with a vision of eternity know the imperishable soul within the body is never sullied by matter, as the sky although everywhere remains untainted. As the sun illuminates the universe, so does the true self illuminate the body with consciousness. Those who see these truths with the eye of knowledge reach the supreme goal."

14

rishna and Arjuna have discussed the predicament *of souls trapped in material bodies. Krishna has emphasized that he dwells in everyone's heart as Supersoul and desires to help embodied souls out of their dilemma if they will only turn to him. Here he reveals how three material qualities called gunas influence an embodied soul's behavior. Arjuna asks how a person behaves once free from such influences and Krishna replies with a brief description of the character and qualities of a liberated soul.[139] He also states that those who love him with heart and soul transcend all material qualities and affirms once again that the benefits of other yogas are contained within bhakti.*

14.1–2 Krishna said, "I shall explain again ultimate knowledge, knowing which sages have reached the highest perfection. Know this, and you will not be reborn.

---

[139] The notion of gunas bears some resemblance to the classic Greek theory of four humors (connected to seasons and earth elements), which were thought to explain personality types. Some debated studies in psychology dating from the 1950s describe personality types ("A" and "B") with traits that resemble the gunas. The subject of gunas is discussed in greater detail in Chapters 17 and 18. See also *gunas* in "Topics in the Gita."

14.3–4 "Arjuna, brahman is the cosmic womb which I impregnate and from which all beings emerge into this world. Of all species, I am the seed-giving father.

14.5–9 "Once in contact with matter, living beings become conditioned by the gunas: *sattva*, *rajas*, and *tamas*. *Sattva* is illuminating, purer than the others. It elevates but also binds souls with an impression of happiness and knowledge. *Rajas*, passion born of desires and urges, binds conditioned beings to an obsession with action. *Tamas*, darkness, arises from lack of knowledge and leads to apathy, madness, and sleep.

14.10–13 "Sometimes one guna dominates behavior, and at other times another dominates.[140]

14.14–18 "Those who die firmly in sattva are reborn in a place of purity and wisdom. Those who die in rajas remain in rajas. Those who die in tamas are reborn in the wombs of bewildered persons or lower species.[141] From

---

[140] By describing embodied beings as subject to three gunas, the Gita does not oversimplify human behavior. The gunas are fluid, constantly mixing, like three primary colors which blend into infinite hues and shades.

[141] A popular impression holds that humans only progress upward through reincarnation, but the Gita states that no one gets to graduate who has not done the homework. Tamasic behavior, for instance, i.e. behavior characterized by a fatalistic lethargy, is best suited to tamasic environments such as other-than-human species and would be out of place in more evolved physical and psychic forms.

sattva comes knowledge, from rajas greed, and from tamas ignorance and confusion.[142]

14.19–20 Those who understand that action in this world is the byproduct of these qualities, and that the true self remains aloof, rise to their original nature, which is the same as mine. They become free from further births and deaths, and in this life such souls live as though tasting nectar."[143]

14.21 Arjuna said, "How do persons who have reached such a state behave, and how do they transcend the gunas?"

14.22–25 Krishna said, "Those who are self-composed and indifferent to disturbance by the gunas, who are steady in happiness and distress, for whom a clod of dirt and a nugget of gold are the same, who treat equally friend and foe—they have transcended the gunas.

---

[142] Earlier (8.6) Krishna described how our frame of mind at the moment of death determines the kind of body we will next inhabit. Here we find indications that the physical location of our next birth is also determined by consciousness at death. This can be geographic (birth on a planet suitable to our psychic disposition) or circumstantial: a sattvic devotional home as described in 6.41, a rajasic goals-oriented environment, or a tamasic environment which may include other than human species.

[143] Krishna's point is that we may behave according to the influence of our personal combination of gunas but we are not their slaves. The Gita seeks to free conditioned souls from the control of the gunas through yoga.

14.26–27 "Those souls who unfailingly offer me their love at once transcend the gunas and achieve brahman. And I am the basis of that brahman, which is immortal, imperishable, and the constitutional position of ultimate happiness."[144]

---

[144] Look at the last verse of each chapter and you will find that Krishna often makes a concluding statement, as here, which summarizes the chapter.

15

rishna's teachings have convinced Arjuna to change his position concerning the battle ahead, and their discussion turns to more intimate topics. Where does the soul go after liberation? What is the nature of the soul's relationship with Krishna in eternity? Krishna hints at the eternal place he calls home, a self-effulgent realm attained by souls who achieve freedom from birth and death. He goes deeper still into a description of his personal nature, emphasizing that he is the ultimate goal hinted at in the original Vedic texts. He expresses his compassion for people struggling in this world and again declares that through yoga they can find him in their heart.

15.1–5 Krishna said, "It is said that entanglement in this world is like the banyan tree, with roots upward and branches downward, without beginning or end, impossible to untangle. This tree of entanglement is fed by the gunas and its twigs are the objects of one's desires. Arjuna, cut down this strongly rooted tree with the axe of detachment, and then seek the place of the Supreme Person from which one never returns. That place is reached by those who are free from duality and pride.[145]

---

[145] Our karmic situation is so complex that it is pointless to attempt to unravel it or understand its origins. Krishna en-

15.6 "That place, my home, needs neither sun nor moon for illumination, and those who go there do not return to this material world.[146]

15.7–11 "The souls in this world are parts of me. They struggle with their senses and mind, carrying conceptions of who they are from one lifetime to the next as the air carries aromas.[147] In each incarnation they obtain senses—hearing and sight, touch and taste and smell— which are grouped around the mind and by which they experience pleasure. Only those who see with the eye of knowledge, those yogis who strive for self-awareness, can understand how a living being can leave all this behind.

15.12–15 "The splendor of the sun and moon and fire, the force which sustains planets in their orbits and nourishes all vegetation, and the digestive ability in all beings— all come from me. Seated in everyone's heart, I am the

---

courages Arjuna to not waste time thinking about how the Kauravas got to be the way they are, or how anyone comes into this world and becomes the way they are. There is a job to do, he says. Focus on that, get it done, and come back to me.

[146] What is fascinating about the vision of a place where liberated souls dwell is that the entire creation—including the eternal world—emanates from Krishna, and Krishna dwells in the hearts of all. In brief, the entire spiritual realm lies within us, which helps to explain how great souls are able to traverse an unpredictable and often dangerous world spreading wisdom: They carry their shelter within them. Detailed descriptions of this eternal realm can be found in the Bhagavata Purana (see "Recommended Readings").

source of remembrance, knowledge, and forgetfulness. I am the author of Vedanta,[148] the knower of the Vedas, and I am also their goal.

15.16–19 "There are two types of beings. Those in this world are fallible, and those in the eternal realm are infallible. Beyond all other beings is the Supreme Soul who enters the three worlds and maintains them. Because I am beyond fallibility and infallibility, the Vedas celebrate me as that Supreme Soul. Those who know me as such know everything and offer me their love.

15.20 "This, Arjuna, is the most confidential part of scriptures and it is revealed by me now. Whoever knows this becomes wise and fulfilled in all they do."

⊚

---

[147] The word *ishvara* in 15.8 is commonly understood as the soul, which moves from one lifetime to the next. The great thirteenth century commentator Madhva (or Madhvacharya) suggests this may also refer to the Supreme Person. By this interpretation, Krishna demonstrates his love for all beings by accompanying them, in his form of paramatma, from birth to birth. This is also described elsewhere in the Gita, as in 18.61: Krishna is present in the hearts of all beings as Supersoul.

[148] Vedanta translates as "end of the Vedas" or their conclusion. Krishna declares that anyone who loves him has reached the conclusion of all scriptural teachings. This ultimate purpose of scripture is so important that Krishna repeats it as the concluding statement of this chapter.

16

he aphorism "it's not what you say but how you say it" applies here. Depending on how we choose to hear him in this chapter, Krishna speaks either with contempt or compassion. Given his declaration of love for all souls and his constant efforts to enlighten them from within their hearts, I read his words here as resonating with concern for all who suffer due to ignorance of their divine nature. Still, his objective is to rouse Arjuna to battle, and we might also imagine Krishna looking across the battlefield and detailing in a strong voice why Arjuna must bring the Kauravas down. We should not misread the stern tone as a cold dividing of souls into good and bad: by definition, all souls reflect the transcendental qualities of the Supreme Being from whom they originate. It is a consequence of their gunas or material conditioning that some souls fall into hurtful behavior. Rather, Krishna is describing a particular and rather extreme category of behavior to which the Kauravas belong: that of asuras, hateful, cruel and arrogant. The obvious asuras make headlines by waging war or committing spectacular crimes; the more insidious asuras live within us. Yoga provides tools for mastering our lower nature so that the sublime qualities of the true self can emerge.

16.1–3 Krishna said, "Qualities of enlightened souls include fearlessness, purity, charity, self-control, self-sacrifice, knowledge of scripture, sincerity, non-violence, truthfulness, peacefulness, compassion for all beings, gentleness, humility, vigor, forgiveness, cleanliness, and lack of envy and pride.

16.4–5 "Those without these qualities—asuras—are proud, arrogant, harsh, and ignorant. While enlightened behavior leads to liberation, the behavior of asuras leads to bondage.

16.6–10 "Asuras do not understand what should be done and not done. Lacking purity, proper behavior and truth, they claim there is no God in control of the world, that it has no reality other than fulfillment of desire.[149] They are lost in such thinking and engage in cruel, hurtful acts that destroy the world.[150] They are deceitful, never satisfied, arrogant, and their illusions lead them to unclean deeds.

16.11–16 "They believe that pleasure to the point of death is all there is, and consequently their anxiety is unlimited. Bound by a network of false hopes and cravings,

---

[149] Indirectly, Krishna is referring to physical reductionist philosophies, which propose that consciousness is generated at some stage of the body's development. Understandably, those who see consciousness as a material byproduct might also see life's purpose as the pursuit of personal success. After all, if there is nothing after death, why hesitate to take whatever we can for ourselves now?

[150] This verse points to a causal connection between belief and the environment, between honoring nature as a manifestation of God and treating nature as a resource for our exploitation.

they earn profits illegally and tell themselves, 'I became rich today, and tomorrow I will do even better.'[151] I defeated my enemies and came out on top. I am successful, powerful, happy, enviable, and because I am also charitable I have every reason to gloat.'[152] They are carried away by such thoughts, snared in their own traps, and fall into a tormented state.

16.17–20 "They follow no authority but themselves. And because they think themselves to be the sole determinant of action they despise me, who am in their hearts and the hearts of all. Such hateful, cruel souls are reborn among like-minded beings and gradually descend into evermore hellish conditions.[153]

---

[151] Fixation on material success stems in large measure from identifying ourself with our work product: The better my company is doing, the better I am doing. We can thank consumer capitalism for this nifty downgrading of self worth.

[152] It is fascinating to note how often charity is offered not from concern for those in need but from a desire for recognition or as a means of rationalizing personal wealth or simply for tax breaks. In the Chapter 18, Krishna gives an overview of mentalities behind acts of charity.

[153] The Gita does not acknowledge the existence of any Evil separate and apart from human consciousness. According to Gita theology, we create our own heaven and hell. Yet taken within the context of Krishna's other teachings, this chapter reveals a striking insight into human nature. Evil, he suggests, refers to souls so deeply entrenched in the gunas that they are always fearful and defensive and consequently aggressive.

16.21–24 "A person who avoids such a life of unbridled desire, anger and greed gradually rises to the supreme goal. Revealed texts should never be abandoned, for they explain how to live without becoming entangled and what to do and not to do in this world."[154]

Like all others, these *asuric* souls actually want to be good but their attempts are self-defeating. Cruel people do not rob their soul of its divinity by being cruel, but they do make it nearly impossible for their divinity to surface because of the harm they do to themselves and to others. Devotional practices can free them from that destructive pathology, although it may take many lifetimes. Elsewhere in the Gita, Krishna describes that he does everything he can to set such deluded souls on a better path but does not interfere with free will. And while he speaks here of facilitating their next birth in an asura family, he does not say this is his preference. Krishna is not a vengeful deity; he does not gloat over the fate of hateful people, but neither will he force anyone to love him. At some point, human beings must take responsibility for their actions and stop blaming God.

[154] Krishna says here that asuras can improve their lives by following scriptural guidelines. His advice to more enlightened individuals (as in 2.42-46) is to not get distracted by scriptural promises of a better life and instead to pursue the ultimate goal of scripture, namely devotion to him.

n the next few moments Arjuna will pick up his weapons and wage war on family, erstwhile friends, and once-honored statesmen. With this in mind, and having just heard Krishna's description of how souls can become deeply enmeshed in the gunas, his question here conveys regret that even people whom we respect can end up disappointing us. Krishna replies, in effect, "What can be done? The Kauravas are responsible for inhumane crimes and must be stopped."Krishna ends the chapter by condemning behavior like the Kauravas' as asat: *false and of no value to anyone.*

17.1 Arjuna said, "What is the fate of people who ignore scripture and worship according to their own faith? Are they conditioned by sattva, rajas, or tamas?"

17.2–5 Krishna said, "Varieties of faith are indeed prompted by a person's gunas or particular conditioning. Believers who are primarily sattvic honor divinities, believers who are dominantly rajasic offer praise to powerful spirits, while believers influenced by a tamasic nature bow to ghosts and the dead.[155]

---

[155] The Gita examines patterns of human behavior and suggests that sattvic people may be attracted to honoring a divine being such as a god, goddess or other creative force. Rajasic

17.6–10 "Everything, even diet, is determined by a person's gunas. A sattvic person is attracted to foods which are wholesome, juicy, appealing, and conducive to good health, happiness, energy and strength. Rajasic persons prefer foods which are bitter, sour, salty and spicy. Such foods burn and cause misery and disease. Tamasic taste favors foods which are stale, flavorless, decomposed and otherwise inedible.

17.11–13 "Sacrifice performed selflessly is sattvic. Sacrifice performed for some selfish motive is rajasic. Sacrifice performed without considering its consequences and without proper formalities such as scriptural direction is tamasic.[156]

17.14–19 "Austerity of body consists of honoring divinities and teachers and remaining non-violent, chaste and

---

people, passionate to achieve worldly success, would understandably be more inspired by a "powerful spirit" such as a captain of industry or Wall Street mogul. Tamasic persons, who may live with depression or suicidal tendencies and for whom disembodied life may appear preferable, might idolize ghosts or the dead. The Sanskrit literature assures us ghosts exist: souls who, because of some misfortune, have not been able to inhabit a physical body but instead move about in subtle bodies.

[156] In general terms, anything we sacrifice—time to promote a social cause, money to support a political candidate, use of our home to host religious gatherings—can fall into one of these three categories. The Gita advises that we consider our deeper motives and the consequences of such gestures before sacrificing any of our resources.

pure. Austerity of speech consists of speaking only the truth and in a manner that is respectful and beneficial to others. Austerity of the mind consists of remaining always calm, self-controlled and pure in purpose. When these three forms of austerity are integrated, such austerity is sattvic. Austerity performed merely for show or to win praise is rajasic. Austerity that is misguided, lacking good purpose, or destructive to oneself or others is tamasic.

17.20–22 "Charity given without condition, at an appropriate time and place, and to a worthy recipient is sattvic. Charity given with expectation of reward or given grudgingly is rajasic. Charity given at the wrong time or place, for the wrong reason, or to an unworthy recipient is tamasic.

17.23–28 "Since the beginning of time, brahmins have performed sacrifices, austerities, and charity by chanting 'OM TAT SAT'[157]—signifying selfless intent and faith in God. It has been this way throughout history; for without faith in God anything done in the name of sacrifice, austerity or charity is devoid of true meaning and useless in this life and the next."

––––––––––––––––––––– ◉ –––––––––––––––––––––

[157] Nothing we do is perfect; everything is subject to the influence of the gunas and even *sattva-guna* carries contaminants of rajas and tamas. Yet when offered to the Supreme Person the imperfections of our acts lose their significance and the devotional intent renders the act sacred. Traditionally brahmins have recited the mantra OM TAT SAT ("The Supreme is all that is") to sanctify actions; more recently, other mantras such as OM NAMO SHIVAYA and HARE KRISHNA have made their way into popular use.

18

 n the final few moments before battle Arjuna acknowledges that he was laboring under a mistaken idea of renunciation. Krishna reassures him again that righteous acts, however difficult, carry no negative karmic effect and constitute true renunciation. He gives brief portraits of workers influenced by the various gunas, their quality of knowledge, determination, and consequent level of happiness; and he reiterates that he dwells in everyone's heart as Supersoul and never abandons anyone who turns to him. The final few verses contain such a moving expression of Krishna's love for his dear friend Arjuna that Sanjaya, who has been channeling the entire dialog for King Dhritarashtra, erupts into tearful ecstasy.

18.1 Arjuna said, "I wish to understand the true sense of *tyaga*, renunciation, and *sannyasa*, the renounced order."

18.2–9 Krishna said, "The wise know that the true meaning of *tyaga* or renunciation is to renounce the mentality of ownership. And they know that living as a true *sannyasi* or renunciant means living without selfish intent.[158] Some say duty itself should be abandoned, but that is not

***

[158] Another way to describe this difference would be to say *sannyasa* means completely giving up (literally "throwing it

my opinion. Neglecting meaningful duty on some illusory pretext is tamasic renunciation. Giving up duty as troublesome or painful is rajasic. Renouncing only the results of duty but still performing duty—that renunciation alone is sattvic.

18.10–12 "Embodied souls can never completely relinquish acting, and so an intelligent person is neither averse to disagreeable acts nor enamored of agreeable acts. For such a true renunciant the usual karmic consequences of work—desirable, undesirable, or mixed—do not occur.[159]

18.13–16 "According to *sankhya* philosophy there are five causes of action: the physical place of action or the body, the agent or self, the tools of action or senses, the different types

———————————————— ◉ ————————————————

all down"), and *tyaga* means generously giving away something one could otherwise have kept.

[159] Occasionally we meet a "true renunciant" or sincere yogi who seems to be confronting troubles of one kind or another. How can we reconcile such suffering with this verse about renunciants escaping karmic reactions? Assuming the yogi is truly selfless and not behaving in a way that would engender fresh karmic reaction, the suffering may be remnants of deeds done long before. My teacher Prabhupada compared such karma to residual spinning of a fan which has been unplugged: The fan is slowing down and will eventually stop. The other explanation of why advanced yogis suffer is that they voluntarily take on the karma of their students, which can sometimes manifest as disease or other troubles. Such voluntary suffering differs from the karmic sufferings of an ordinary person.

of action, and the Supreme Person. Whatever a person does with body, mind or speech depends on all of these. Consequently, those who think themselves the sole determinant of action think in a manner unwise and shallow.

18.17 "Those who see things with intelligence cleansed of ego, even if obligated to kill, incur no karmic consequences by such duty.[160]

18.18–22 "Knowledge which recognizes the imperishable essence of all beings, whatever their particular species, is sattvic.[161] Knowledge which judges each living be-

---

[160] The phrase *na ahankrita*, "not motivated by ego," separates whimsical acts from acts sanctioned by valid authority. Of course, how to determine "valid authority" deserves a book of its own. In Arjuna's case, his engagement in battle has been authorized by scriptural injunction, civil law, learned counsel, and Krishna himself. But these may appear arbitrary. How is Arjuna's commitment to fight different from that of martyrs who kill in the name of God? What distinguishes a hero from a terrorist? Briefly, the Gita points to a normative cosmic architecture or universal morality, which serves as framework for justice. In modern terminology, the Gita favors natural law over positive law, natural law being a fundamental standard of human behavior that overrides any nation's political, military, or religious agenda. Some of this is addressed in Satya P. Agarwal's book *The Social Message of the Gita: Symbolized as Lokasamgraha* (Delhi: Motilal Banarsidass, 1995).

[161] Clearly, knowing all beings to be eternal souls does not mean excusing their hurtful behavior. Krishna is encouraging Arjuna to fight the Kauravas, not let them get away with

ing as unrelated to others is rajasic. And knowledge which leads a person to ignore all others and to obsess over work that has no lasting significance is tamasic.

18.23–25 "Action performed with discipline and without selfish motive is sattvic. Action performed out of ego and for personal benefit is rajasic. Action performed out of routine, with no regard for its consequences or the harm it may cause, is tamasic.[162]

18.26–28 "A worker who is selfless, determined, enthusiastic, and unaffected by success or failure is sattvic. A worker who is aggressive, emotional, envious, and greedy for gain is rajasic. A worker who finds fault with others, who procrastinates and is undisciplined, obstinate, and lazy is tamasic.

18.29–32 "Understanding that distinguishes what to do from what not to do, what to fear from what not to fear, what binds from what liberates is sattvic. Understanding

———————————————⊛———————————————

their crimes. It is how to fight them that Krishna wishes Arjuna to see: with a strong but compassionate hand. There is a right way and a wrong way for all things, including conduct in battle. International law has always sought this right way by balancing necessity and humanity. Necessity says that if someone attacks, you are justified in doing whatever is needed to protect yourself and your home. Humanity dictates that in the pursuit of necessity harm must be minimized as far as possible. Viewing an enemy with compassion can be an effective barometer for achieving that balance.

[162] An obvious example is fasting. When moderate, for instance as part of a yogic practice, fasting is sattvic. When aggres-

which cannot distinguish what is dharma from what is not dharma, or what should be done or not done—such understanding is rajasic. And understanding that confuses dharma with *adharma* is tamasic.

18.33–35 "Determination which is unbreakable, which is sustained by yoga practice, and which regulates the mind, breath and senses is sattvic. Determination directed at acquiring wealth and pleasure is rajasic. And determination which cannot rise above dreams, sleep, fear, depression and regret—such determination is tamasic.

18.36–39 "Happiness which tastes like poison in the beginning but like nectar at the end and which awakens the quest for self-awareness is sattvic.[163] Happiness which tastes like nectar in the beginning but like poison at the end and which comes from the interaction of senses and sense objects is rajasic. And happiness which is blind to self-realization and arises from laziness, illusion and sleep is tamasic.

———————————— ❖ ————————————

sive, perhaps to look sexy, fasting is rajasic. When extreme, for example as an act of despair, fasting is tamasic. These are generalizations concerning the gunas and there are always exceptions. For example, Krishna spoke the Gita to get Arjuna angry—usually considered a rajasic emotion—at a time when anger was needed to fight with determination.

[163] This is a good description of some spiritual practices. As a young bhakta living in ashrams, I remember thinking about the next morning's cold shower with dread. With time, those bracing, exhilarating showers actually became pleasant. Call me crazy, or try it yourself.

18.40–44 "No one anywhere escapes these three gunas of material nature. A brahmin is by nature equal to all, calm, pure, honest, wise and faithful to the Supreme Person. A *kshatriya* is by nature heroic, powerful, disciplined, courageous, generous and in command. The natural disposition of *vaishyas* is toward agriculture, cow protection and commerce; and the vocational inclination of *shudras* is to serve others.[164]

18.45–47 "You can reach perfection by pursuing a vocation appropriate to your skills. This is done by offering your work as a service to God, and thus it is better to do what suits your nature even imperfectly than attempt the work of another even if done well. There is never any fault in pursuing what matches your abilities.[165]

---

[164] In ancient India, *shudras* (members of the artist/artisan/laborer class) were never subjugated or considered inferior. The *Rig-Veda* describes the shudra class as emanating from the feet of the Supreme Being; and while this may seem a put-down, from the bhakti perspective a place at the Supreme Being's feet is an exalted position and one which is coveted by the most advanced yogis. Since shudras provide society with essential services, they are credited with supporting the rest of the social body (brahmin head, kshatriya arms, and vaishya stomach).

[165] Humans are complex creatures; how are we to know what vocation is "appropriate to your skills"? (See "Topics in the Gita" for more on the various kinds of dharma.) Birthright is not a dependable indicator; someone born to dentist parents will not necessarily make a good dentist. Formerly, gurus

"Those who know me return to me."

were in a good position to make vocational recommendations since they saw their students every day and could evaluate their character and propensities. Parents in traditional Indian culture also consulted astrologers, who would offer advice about a child's career prospects. These days the er-

18.48–49 "Nor should you ever abandon what is right for you since every effort is flawed, just as fire is covered by smoke.[166] Approach your duty objectively, without regard for personal profit, and you shall achieve the highest goals of renunciation.

18.50–54 "I wish to tell you, Arjuna, in summary how a person achieves the summit of self-realization. With pure intellect; with functions of mind, body and words subdued; with attraction and aversion equally mastered; with diet regulated; with constant devotion to yoga and meditation; devoid of pride and anger and ego; and with a peaceful heart—a person with these qualities, who is one with brahman,[167] wholly joyful, purged of all regret, and equal toward all creatures, that one is my beloved and reaches the heights of self-awareness.

18.55–56 "In truth, those who offer me their love come to know me. And those who know me in truth return

---

ratic job market forces people to take whatever is available and then figure out by trial and error if they can live with it. Lately, some agencies have emerged which understand that work can be a part of life's full spiritual experience (the Spirit in Business Institute and the Association for Spirit at Work, among others). Mythologist Joseph Campbell would advise his students, "Follow your bliss." The Gita's position on career planning is elegantly simple: take guidance from a realized teacher (4.34), and whatever you do, do it with devotion (9.27).

[166] "Perfection" from the bhakti perspective includes imperfection, as it is our "flaws" that render us unique individuals.

to me. Though preoccupied with various activities, such souls are protected by me, and by my grace they return to my eternal, imperishable home.

18.57–60 "In everything you do depend on me, take shelter in me, think of me. By my grace you shall overcome all obstacles. If you do not hear me and withdraw from battle, thinking yourself the sole agent of action, then you will be lost. Your nature will compel you to act, even against your will.

18.61–62 "All beings move about like passengers seated on machines made of maya. Their movements are directed by the Supreme Being who dwells in their hearts. Give yourself over to that Supreme Being in your heart and by his grace you shall know ultimate peace and eternal rest.

For a while, when traveling by plane, Prabhupada would pin a crayon drawing of Krishna to the seat in front of him as a visual meditation while chanting on his japa beads. A young child had given him the drawing as a gift. It was a simple stick figure, artistically flawed, but a masterpiece of devotion. This verse encourages us to not overly judge our effort by superficial material standards. The Supreme Person sees the love with which something is done.

[167] For bhakti yogis, "one with Brahman" refers to the loving solidarity of the individual soul's interests with those of the Supreme Person, not the negation of selfhood envisioned by some Advaita Vedanta schools (see "Topics in the Gita" for more on Advaita philosophy).

18.63 "I have offered you this gift of most confidential knowledge. Reflect, and then do what you think best.[168]

18.64–65 "Just hear this from me. I am speaking to you because I love you and wish for you the greatest good. Always think of me, love me, and act from that love. Without the least doubt, you shall come to me. I promise you this, for you are my dear friend.

18.66 "Set aside consideration for any other dharma and accept me as your shelter.[169] I will protect you from all consequences. Have no fear.[170]

---

[168] There are no "thou shalts" or "thou shalt nots" in the Gita. The closest Krishna comes to a direct order is 18.66, where he promises "Surrender to me, and if you do then I will protect you." Rather than insisting on blind obedience, the Gita encourages dialogue, questioning, and the exercise of best judgment. This civilized policy not only honors innate human intelligence, but also reveals God's plan for the world as a respectful cooperation in fulfilling the work of creation.

[169] The words *saranam vraja* mean "take refuge," but I was always curious about the word *vraja*, which is also a synonym for Vrindavan, Krishna's village. During his visit to Paris in 1973, I asked Prabhupada whether we might understand this verse as meaning "take shelter of me as I am in Vrindavan." He thought for a moment and then said, "Yes, it can be understood in that way." Some scholars would no doubt roll their eyes at this blatantly bhakti interpretation of the Gita's *charama-shloka*, or essential verse. Swami B.V. Tripurari provides an excellent insight into Krishna's word choices in his

"I am firm in my resolve and will act as you have advised."

---

commentary *Bhagavad Gita: Its Feeling and Philosophy* (San Rafael, CA: Mandala Publishing Group, 2001).

[170] In this extraordinary verse, Krishna offers unqualified assurance that we have nothing to fear by embarking on the journey to enlightenment. As radical a departure as that journey may be from the life we have known to this moment, Krishna's unconditional guarantee is that we will not be di-

18.67–69 "This should not to be revealed to anyone who lacks discipline or who is not a bhakta, or to anyone who envies me.[171] Certainly, anyone who shares these secrets with my devotees will come to me without doubt. For there is none as dear to me as they, nor will there ever be anyone dearer to me than they.[172]

18.70–71 "Those who study this sacred conversation worship me with their intellect, and those who listen with an open mind achieve liberation and shall dwell among pure souls in worlds of bliss.

---

minished or left stranded by setting out. This verse is wonderful for another reason as well. Elsewhere, Krishna declares himself to be the source of the Vedic scriptures (15.15) which define and regulate *dharma*, or righteous behavior. He even warns of the risk in ignoring such scriptural law (16.23), yet here he overrides his own admonition by saying, "If you love me and act purely from that love, then you have reached the summit of all dharma and everything else will be taken care of by me." Herbie Hancock once described jazz as a calling in which "the really good stuff happens outside the safety zone" (*Possibilities*, Magnolia Home Entertainment, 2005). At some point in our spiritual evolving, we have to leave the safety zone of the world we know. Here Krishna promises his help if we take that risk on his behalf. This verse is considered by many scholars to be the Gita's *charama-shloka*: its "ultimate statement." Schweig does something marvelous by pushing the *charama-shloka* back to 18.64, where Krishna tells Arjuna why he chose him to receive these teachings: "You are so much loved by me! Therefore I shall speak for your well-being." (Schweig, pp. 276–78)

18.72 "O Arjuna, have you heard me? Have I held your attention? Are your ignorance and illusion gone?"[173]

18.73 Arjuna said, "Yes, my illusion is gone and I have regained my memory by your grace. My doubts have been erased. I am firm in my resolve and will act as you have advised."

18.74–77 Sanjaya said, "O King, I have heard this extraordinary conversation and I am in ecstasy. It is by the grace of my guru Vyasa[174] that I am witness to this supreme secret of yoga as revealed personally to Arjuna by

---

[171] The risk is self-evident in promoting the idea that we can give up all dharmas because God has promised to protect us. Giving up socially acceptable behavior leads to chaos. Krishna implies here that persons not yet prepared for enlightenment—persons who lack self-discipline, devotion, and faith—will tend to misinterpret his teachings for selfish ends. As Antonio warns in *Merchant of Venice*, "The Devil can cite Scripture for his purpose." Be cautious, Krishna says to Arjuna, that you not inadvertently encourage fanaticism by attempting to instruct people who may not be ready to properly understand spiritual teachings.

[172] In the previous verses, Krishna cautioned against revealing the Gita to those who are not ready for enlightenment. Who then is ready? *Bhaktim mayi*: "Those who have offered me their love." The distinction is clarifying. Krishna is not seeking missionaries to go out and convert nonbelievers. In fact, he says leave those people alone. The ones who have his interest are those who are already inclined to love him.

the master of yoga Krishna. O King, I am recalling this wondrous conversation over and over and feeling bliss without end. I remember seeing the magnificent form of Krishna and I am struck with wonder and rejoice again and again.

18.78 "Where there is Krishna, master of all mystic yoga, and where there is the mighty archer Arjuna, there is fortune, victory, well-being and righteousness. That is my opinion."[175]

---

[173] After two hours of intense dialogue and a never-before-seen revelation of the Universal Form, there is something tongue-in-cheek about Krishna asking whether he has held Arjuna's attention. We might read a note of affectionate humor here.

[174] Vyasadeva, Sanjaya's guru, is credited with having been the first to codify Vedic wisdom in written form.

[175] Dhritarashtra did not ask Sanjaya for his opinion, but Sanjaya is offering it anyway perhaps inspired by Krishna telling Arjuna to "do what you think best." In effect, his opinion declares to Dhritarashtra that his sons do not represent righteousness, that they have visited only misery on their kingdom, and that they will without doubt lose the war. Sanjaya's exuberant response to what he has seen and heard reveals something of the love for Krishna that has awakened in his own heart after bearing witness to this historic discussion.

AFTERWORD

After his transformation, Arjuna picks up his bow and arrows and prepares to fight. Seeing him rally, the Pandava warriors roar their approval. They blow conches, beat drums, and create a deafening noise. Demigods assemble from various quarters of the universe to watch the battle. Eighteen horrible, bloody days later the Pandavas win the war, but they incur losses that are never remedied.

Arjuna's oldest brother Yudhishthira is installed as king but lives the rest of his life in guilt over the catastrophic number of lives sacrificed on the battlefield. The kingdom itself never recovers from the fratricidal war, and eventually (thirty-six years after war's end) the remaining family members destroy themselves in a fit of retributive madness. The "victory of good over evil" which the battle was meant to symbolize fails to stave off the onset of Kali Yuga, the current Age of Quarrel, and the reign of enlightened kings comes to an end.

How should we understand this disappointing conclusion to the Mahabharata story? Perhaps we are meant to see that bhakti, or any yoga for that matter, does not always result well materially. Yoga aims at reawakening our identity as eternal souls and igniting the love that unites us with the Supreme Person. The life that comes with that reawakening is often very different from the life we may have wanted for ourselves. Yet according to the Gita anything undertaken in the spirit of bhakti is de facto a success, irrespective of its material outcome, as it brings us closer to the Supreme Person in our heart.

The kshatriya code of honor dictates that true warriors should not die at home like house pets. At the end of his reign, Yudhishthira passes the crown to Arjuna's grandson Pariksit, and the four Pandava brothers and their wife Draupadi set out on foot for the Himalayas. All but Yudhishthira die along the way, and each gains entrance into the eternal realm. There is a lovely story at the very end of the epic. Yudhishthira continues traveling north, his only companion an old dog who had been a faithful mascot to the Pandavas during their Himalayan pilgrimage. As he approaches the summit, Yudhishthira encounters Indra, king of the gods, who invites him to enter the eternal realm as reward for a lifetime of devotion.

"However," Indra says, "there is no place in heaven for the dog."

Yudhishthira thinks back on the suffering caused by people who should have known better, people who possessed not an ounce of the faith his dog had shown. He thanks Indra for the offer, turns, and prepares to head off with his companion trotting by his side. At that moment the dog reveals himself to be Yama, Lord of Death. Moved by Yudhishthira's choice to honor a dog over his own salvation, Yama invites him to join his family in the eternal realm.

❧

The Gita is not about bringing down evil; it is about lifting our soul to levels we never thought possible. At the start of the Gita, Arjuna is ego-driven and paralyzed by fear and uncertainty due to misidentifying with material limitations. By the end of the Gita he is soul-driven,

*The Gita is a call for souls to love Krishna,
seen here with Radha, the embodiment of devotion*

Krishna's inspiration provides Arjuna the self-confidence to embrace a painful dharma.

energized, at peace with himself, and confident of his ability to accomplish what had seemed like an impossible dharma. Initially, he mistook his assignment as lacking any redemptive qualities, as nothing but a cruel task at odds with his compassionate nature and everyone's best interests. Still, his love for Krishna enabled him to consider a very different point of view, namely that if a painful task is undertaken in the spirit of bhakti—that is, not with vengeance or disgust but with devotion—then even war could be devotional service.

As extreme as Arjuna's dilemma may be, his discussion with Krishna is for our benefit for it reveals that nothing exists outside the arena of our journey to selfhood. Everything, however painful, has meaning deeper than what our senses and mind perceive. And that meaning is Gita: the call of the Supreme Person to join him in loving devotion.

Topics

in the

Gita

Advaita Vedanta – Literally "the nondual conclusion of the Vedas," this monistic school founded by Shankaracharya (also called Adi Shankara, 788–820) holds that all of creation is a single reality, one supreme formless energy which sages call *brahman* and in which everything resides. Advaita, nonduality, proposes that all beings souls are identical with this formless energy. By this definition the *jiva-atma*, or individual soul, is equal to and not different from the *paramatma*, or God. One of Shankara's famous quotes says *brahma satyam jagat mithya jivo brahmaiva naparah*: "*Brahman* is the only truth, the world is illusion, and there is ultimately no difference between *brahman* and the individual self." Impersonal philosophy is tempting as it represents freedom from the anxiety and responsibility of personhood, which is often painful. Still, the Gita calls impersonal meditation *duhkham*, "troublesome" (12.5); and while not denying that some souls seek undifferentiated oneness with impersonal *brahman*, Krishna declares that the happiness from such oneness is inferior to the happiness of his loving service.

Ahimsa – The avoidance of violence (*a-himsa*). This term is sometimes misunderstood as pacifism. The Gita exalts *ahimsa* as a moral virtue, but not one to be exercised at the expense of acting for a righteous cause such as Arjuna reclaiming his kingdom from malicious usurpers.

Anger – *Krodha*, anger, arising from *rajo-guna* (the mode of passion) is considered a toxic emotion that pollutes the mind and body. Along with *lobha* (greed) and *kama* (craving or selfish desire), anger is one of the three strongest anchors binding the soul to repeated birth and death. Still, righteous anger should not be artificially suppressed. A simple anecdote underscores this principle. Prabhupada was with an assistant in Vrindavan in the early 1970s, when a mosquito sneaked inside the netting around his bed. The assistant wanted to chase the mosquito away, but Prabhupada stopped him. "In Vrindavan," he said, "even the mosquitoes are devotees and should not be disturbed." Then the mosquito landed on Prabhupada's arm and stung him. "He has attacked," Prabhupada said. "Now you can get him." His point was that anger is justified when in response to aggression.

Atma – Depending on the context, this critical term may refer to the body, mind, intellect, or the Supreme Person, but its most frequent meaning is the individual soul. The *atma*, or eternal self (also called *jiva-atma* or finite soul, as opposed to *paramatma* or Supreme Soul), is literally who we are before, during, and after our birth in a material body. Evidence of the *atma*'s presence is conscious awareness, which permeates our body the way heat and light permeate a room in which a fire burns. The Gita's second chapter describes the *atma* as indestructible, eternal, unsullied by matter, and always a person. Advaita Vedanta or *mayavada*, philosophy, offers a partial understanding of the *atma* by describing it as the same as God. *Mayavada* doctrine contends that after enlightenment the *atma* sheds the illusion of personhood and again "becomes one" or merges with the totality of *brahman*. This partial understanding of the soul's nature is completed by the Gita, which adds the critical definition of each soul as an individual distinct being. "Oneness" according to the Gita is oneness of interest and qualities, not quantity.

AUM – According to the Upanishads, AUM (also spelled OM) is the primordial sound of creation, the vibration that set the universe in motion. The word comprises the first and last vowels ("A" and "U") as well as the last consonant ("M") of the Sanskrit alphabet. AUM thus encompasses all truths that words can convey. A second interpretation of AUM's component parts equates "A" with waking consciousness, "U" with the dream state, and "M" with deep sleep—or, taken together, the sum total of all consciousness. According to the *bhakti* tradition, "A" refers to Krishna (who says in Gita 10.33 that he is represented by the letter "A"); "U" refers to Radha, the embodiment of devotion; and "M" refers to all souls, who are united with Krishna through devotion. By this definition, AUM embodies the relationship of love, which unites all souls with the Supreme Soul.

Bhagavan – *Bhakti* theology holds that God manifests in three ways: as the impersonal *brahman* energy; as *paramatma* or the Supreme Being situated in everyone's heart; and as Bhagavan, the original Supreme Person who is the source of both *brahman* and *paramatma*. His eternal (*sat*) nature can be perceived in *brahman* and his all cognizant nature (*chit*) in *paramatma*. Only in his original form of Bhagavan can his all-blissful nature (*ananda*) be known.

Bhagavata Purana – This Sanskrit history (*purana*) describes itself as the "ripened fruit of Vedic wisdom." Among the eighteen principal *puranas*, the Bhagavata provides intimate details concerning Krishna's life and interaction with his loving devotees, forming in essence a post-graduate study of the Gita. In the Gita, Krishna's final encouragement to Arjuna is to set aside his concerns for any dharma other than loving him. But what happens from that point on? Where does the soul in love with Krishna go after death? What are the activities of such a soul in eternity? These are among the subjects treated in the Bhagavata Purana.

Bhakti – More than a passive awareness of the Supreme Being, *bhakti* refers to devotional service or the active demonstration of love. The root *bhaj* means to serve or worship and also to participate or share. In *bhakti*, every deed, word, and thought is enacted with conscious intent to please the Supreme Person. A second root, *bhanj*, signifies separation and suggests that love requires two distinct persons, the lover and the beloved. Scholars of India's yoga traditions sometimes define *bhakti* as separate and apart from the two other principal yoga paths, *jnana* (study) and *karma* (work); but the Gita positions *bhakti* more accurately as the fulfillment of these other disciplines. Real *jnana* or knowledge leads to an understanding of the soul and its loving relationship with the Supreme Person (7.19), and the noblest form of *karma* is service rendered not in expectation of return but as an offering of love (2.51). *Bhakti* is also the only form of yoga which extends past liberation. While other yogas benefit a soul's evolution through lifetimes in the material world, *bhakti* is the activity of the soul in eternity. There is no difference between loving devotional service performed in a material body or in the liberated state. The means and the end in *bhakti* are one and the same.

Brahma – India's creation narrative says that at the birth of the universe the first being to appear is called Brahma. There are unlimited universes and a Brahma in each universe. All these Brahmas are exalted souls charged with the responsibility of completing creation, i.e., populating the planets and establishing cosmic order. Krishna refers to Brahma in the Gita (2.16), stating that even such an exalted being is eventually subject to death in this material world.

Brahman – This word should not be confused with *brahmin,* which refers to a male or female member of India's priest class; or with Brahma, the first created being. *Brahman* is the energy of which all creation is constituted. *Brahman* is the foundation of both the temporary material and eternal transcendent worlds. Everything that exists is made of *brahman,* either in its original pure state of complete consciousness or in its temporary state covered by illusion (*maya*), which is called matter. A famous Sanskrit aphorism (in the *Brihadaranyaka-Upanishad*) states *aham brahmasmi*: "I am *brahman,*" meaning that we living beings are also constituted of *brahman* energy. The Gita nonetheless distinguishes between the individual finite *brahman* souls who can forget their eternal nature and the unlimited Supreme Brahman or Krishna who never forgets. The Gita declares (14.27) that Krishna is the basis of *brahman.*

Devas – Literally "godlike," India's wisdom texts describe *devas,* "demigods," as empowered beings entrusted with regulating air, light, water, and other natural functions. Honoring these administrators of universal affairs with *yajnas,* or sacrifices, has several benefits. Worshipers developed a relationship with nature and ultimately with the Supreme Person behind nature. Honoring *devas* nurtures a sense of responsibility to the Earth and its resources. Eventually, the devotion fostered by these rituals leads to recognition that the *devas* derive their powers from an even higher source, the Supreme Person.

Dharma – From the root *dhr* to uphold or sustain, *dharma* refers to righteous behavior that "sustains" the world. We are responsible for many *dharmas* in the course of a lifetime: *kula-dharma*, family duties; *jati-dharma*, community obligations; *sva-dharma*, vocational duties based on our unique personal skills; and others. These duties have both external and internal purpose. The external purpose is to maintain the smooth functioning of society; the internal purpose or "essence of *dharma*" as Krishna calls it (12.20 and also 18.66) is to remember him and love him. From the Gita's perspective, love for the Supreme Person is the ultimate duty or *sanatana-dharma*, the eternal *dharma* of all beings. As water is by nature liquid, as sugar is sweet or fire hot, the *dharma* or natural condition of all souls is the state of love for the Supreme Being.

Ego – *Ahankara*, the ego referred to in 2.69, is our mistaken identification with the body-mind vehicle. This material or false ego compels us to put ourselves and our personal interests at the center of attention. Yoga practice does not aim at negating ego altogether (the permanent ego or *atma* cannot in any case be negated since it is indestructible), but at cultivating real ego or awareness of ourselves as the soul which animates the body. The symptoms of such awareness are humility, selfless service, and other refined qualities described in 12.13–20.

Gopis – Young cowherd women of Krishna's village Vrindavan. The *gopis* display *madhurya-rasa*, conjugal affection, the most intimate form of love for the Supreme Person. This sentiment of conjugal love does not figure in the Gita, which concerns itself with the basic lessons of spiritual life.

Gunas – The three qualities of material nature: *sattva* (goodness or light), *rajas* (passionate action), and *tamas* (ignorance or darkness). The *gunas* are determinants of behavior, the three general moods displayed by all embodied beings. All souls are subject to influence by the *gunas* until reaching full self-awareness. The *gunas* combine to create an unlimited variety of character traits. No one, for instance, is completely *sattvic*; there is always a tinge of *rajas* and *tamas*. Animals also behave according to the *gunas*, although there are no karmic consequences to their behavior.

Guru – A learned teacher, literally "heavy with knowledge." There are many types of gurus: military, culinary, musical, scriptural—every field of knowledge has its men and women gurus or learned teachers. In the domain of yoga instruction gurus are of two main kinds: *diksha-gurus* who award initiation to qualified students, and *shiksha-gurus* who offer instruction that supports the teachings of the *diksha-guru* but who do not themselves initiate. Traditionally, students may have many *shiksha-gurus* but only one *diksha -guru*. The *bhakti* tradition does not acknowledge self-made gurus. The *Mundaka-Upanishad* (1.2.13) describes the qualifications of a guru: *shrotriya*, learned in scripture and recognized by an authorized preceptorial line (*parampara*); and *brahma-nishtha*, self-realized and able to teach by example. The Gita stipulates that candidates for initiation should serve such a guru with humility and ask relevant questions in order to remove all doubts (4.34).

Jnana – *Jnana,* or knowledge, forms the foundation of progressive human life. *Jnana* is not an accumulation of data; rather it is the growing awareness through study and reflection of life as a purposeful experience leading to a tangible goal: the reawakening of spiritual consciousness. The Gita does not condemn *jnana,* although at times Krishna is critical of those who pursue *jnana* independent of its true goal. The Gita differentiates between *jnana* and *vijnana* (realized versus applied knowledge). *Vijnana* implies knowledge that has been incorporated into behavior—the difference, for example, between espousing nonviolence as a worthy idea and living a nonviolent life.

Karma – This term refers to development of material bodies and anything that binds the soul to repeated birth in material bodies. The word is used to identify action or work, the effect of such work, and also the law governing action and its effects. The Gita describes that karmic reactions can be desirable, undesirable, or mixed (18.12). The notion of desirable or "good" karma is misleading since good deeds also bind the performer to the material world. Someone performing charitable work, for instance, must return in another lifetime to enjoy the results.

Karmic reactions have three stages of growth. *Prarabdha* refers to ripe, manifested reactions, i.e., consequences that can be seen, starting with the body we currently inhabit. Desirable *prarabdha* might include wealth, beauty, fame, power, and other forms of affluence. Undesirable *prarabdha* might include legal problems, health issues, relationship breakups, financial woes, or work-related disappointments. Because it is already in progress, *prarabdha* is hard if not impossible to change. *Sanchitta* refers to karmic reactions in seed form, the not-yet-manifested consequences of past deeds. Making amends, asking forgiveness from someone we have harmed, or doing community service in a place we have damaged can still stop these reactions. *Agama* refers to future reactions to what we are doing now, conditions that might not emerge for several lifetimes. These are easiest to counteract through such efforts as yoga, study, and change of behavior.

Karma has three arenas of activity: thoughts, words, and deeds. There are reactions on all three levels. There is less karma for thoughts, but thoughts lead to words and deeds that engender more serious reactions. The Gita recommends catching harmful thoughts before they evolve into words or deeds (2.62–63). Words are a more obvious breeding ground for karmic reaction. A dictator may never lift a gun, for example, and cause harm solely with the power of words. The most obvious arena of karmic activity is action: climate change comes easily to mind.

Karma raises troubling questions. Can we really rationalize as karmic justice infant mortality, sexual abuse, or madmen with guns running amok in offices and restaurants? Are these all instruments of destiny? In reaction to the tragedies revealed in the Universal Form, Arjuna admits his inability to fathom the complex workings of material nature and does not allow the apparent injustice of karma to undermine his faith. Instead he focuses on what he knows, namely that there is a battle to be fought, and renews his commitment to doing what he can to make the world as livable as possible for others.

One form of action engenders no karmic consequences (*akarma*): *bhakti*, or devotional service. Whatever reactions might otherwise have resulted, an act performed selflessly and out of love for the Supreme Person takes place in a karma-free arena (4.16-23).

Love – When we imagine love as something we need but do not have and have to get, it saps our energy and compromises our ability to think clearly. When we understand love as the normative condition of life, the permanent relationship between the individual soul and the Supreme Soul, then it energizes us, allows us to transcend material limitations, and facilitates clear thinking. In our conditioned state, what we call love dissipates when the conditions we place on it are not fulfilled. The Gita encourages a different view of what we are: indestructible beings whose ultimate object of love is permanently in our heart (18.61).

Maya – "That which is not," *maya* is the forgetfulness which leads conditioned souls to mistakenly identify with their temporary body and mind. The indestructible soul is not actually changed by *maya*, but under its influence souls move about in a dreamlike condition thinking "I am male (or female), I am old (or young), tall (or short), wise (or foolish), black (or white), Asian (or American)," *ad infinitum*. Yoga helps souls conditioned by *maya* to withdraw their attention from the temporary external world and focus within. With practice, yoga counteracts the influence of *maya* and awakens consciousness of the original eternal self.

Mind – The mind, as identified in the Gita, is the databank that collects sensory input before it goes to the intelligence for assessment and possible action. It is the repository of all our sensory impressions and the

Krishna's mother Devaki and father Vasudeva gaze upon their divine child, the Supreme Being in personal form (saguna brahman).

place where thoughts, feelings, and desires are generated. The mind itself is not intelligent; it merely gathers data and then accepts or rejects the data. Its operations are mechanical, carrying its impressions "as the air carries aromas" (15.8). In order to do its job, the mind must be free to gather and combine impressions and experiences accumulated throughout life. As a consequence, the mind is free-spirited and capable of generating potentially harmful behavior.

The Upanishads offer the analogy of a chariot, in which the horses are the senses, the mind is the reigns, and intelligence is the driver. Ideally the mind should be disciplined by the intelligence, which tells it how to channel its sensory impressions for useful ends. The first goal of yoga is to calm the agitations of the mind (*chitta-vrittis*), a benefit also derived from chanting a *mantra* (*manas*-mind, *traya*-liberation). Arjuna expresses his inability to control his mind, which he describes as restless as the wind. Krishna reassures him that it is possible with practice and discipline (6.34–35). Another function of the mind is to carry the soul at death to its next body (8.6).

Nirguna – Literally 'without qualities," this word is used to describe the source of all creation as a formless energy. In many Advaita Vedanta schools, merging with this formless energy constitutes the soul's ultimate liberation. There is something appealing in the notion of merging into an eternal formless energy and divesting ourselves of all responsibility, but the Gita has a thing or two to say about *nirguna* starting with 12.2–8: Meditating on formlessness is a difficult yogic path. The Gita also declares that *nirguna* represents only a partial understanding of reality since the individuality of each soul is inviolable (2.10–24). As if to underscore the centrality of personhood in the fulfillment of yoga, Krishna ends Chapter 14 with an unequivocal declaration that he, the Supreme Being, is the foundation of *brahman* and its very source.

OM – See AUM.

Paramatma – One of the main topics of the Gita is Krishna's "localized" feature, *paramatma* or supreme (*param*) soul (*atma*), who resides in the heart of all beings as observer and friend. *Paramatma* is the source of inspiration, the inner voice of wisdom in all beings.

Parampara – India's wisdom teachings have been passed down since before recorded history in a succession of teachers called the guru *parampara*. Each school of Indian philosophy has its particular *parampara* lineage. The *bhakti* school ascribes the beginning of its guru lineage to the Supreme Person himself. At the dawn of creation the Supreme Being inspired Brahma, the first being in the universe, with Veda or original knowledge. Brahma taught the Veda to his son Narada, who entrusted it to Vyasadev, who is credited with having compiled Vedic knowledge in written form. Gita 4.1–2 describes that the *parampara* succession was broken over the course of time and that Krishna now reestablishes the lineage through Arjuna.

Prakriti – This term refers to the elements which make up material creation. *Prakriti* is inert: It only operates when life is present to animate the elements of creation. Consequently living beings themselves are also referred to as *prakriti*.

Rasa – The *bhakti* tradition describes love for God as taking place in evolving stages called *rasas*, or tastes. According to Rupa Goswami's sixteenth century treatise *Bhakti-rasamrita-sindhu*, all souls have an eternal loving relationship with the Supreme Being (called the soul's *svarupa* or specific form). The practice of *bhakti-yoga* revives awareness of that *svarupa*, and in their more developed stage *bhakti-yogis* are able to perceive themselves in that eternal form.

Rupa Goswami compares the early stage of love for God to sugarcane juice: liquid and pure but easily shaken. This early stage is called *shanta-rasa*, a peaceful but passive knowledge of God's presence. *Shanti*, or peace, is certainly desirable in a violent world, but it is only the beginning in the unfolding of love for the Supreme Person. When stimulated by a desire to actively demonstrate love, this peaceful stage grows into *dasya-rasa*, or servitude. Rupa Goswami compares this sentiment to cane juice boiled and thickened into syrup. Servitude implies higher and lower stations. When that distinction disappears, love between equals emerges. This is *sakhya-rasa*, the mood of friendship with God, which is compared to syrup thickened further into molasses. When friends interact, they treat each other casually. When the *bhakta* sheds that informality in order to pay closer attention to Krishna's needs, such love is called *vatsalya-rasa* or parental affection. The qualifier in parental love is its sense of duty toward the child. In its most intense stage, love for Krishna sheds all sense of duty and what remains is reckless, ecstatic love, which cares nothing for social conventions. This is *madhurya-rasa*, conjugal affection. The *gopis*, or cowherd women of Vrindavan, display this highest level of love, which is compared to molasses hardened into solid rock candy. Arjuna is in a relationship with Krishna that blends friendship and servitude. In 2.7, Arjuna demonstrates his desire for Krishna's guidance by saying, "Now I am your disciple. Please instruct me." In effect, he is setting aside the casual nature of their friendship in order to benefit from the more formal relationship of student and guru.

Sadhu – A *sadhu* or saint is someone who embodies eternal life (*sat*). Stories of men, women, and children *sadhus* fill *bhakti* texts such as Bhagavata Purana.

Saguna – Literally "with qualities," this term is used to define the source of all existence as a person endowed with form and personality. Krishna declares himself in the Gita to be that Supreme Person who is the source of all creation. Historically, there have been objections to the proposition that the source of everything possesses shape and character. To some, worship of a personal divinity is idolatrous and simplistic. To others accepting Krishna as the unique person behind creation is sectarian and exclusionary. Still others such as the Advaitins argue that form exists only in the temporal world. While the Gita replies to each of these arguments, intuition tells me that a larger objection stops people from accepting the notion of a personal God: Relationships are hard work and often painful. Why would we subject ourselves to that discomfort eternally? Krishna reassures us that loving him will not end in a broken heart but in a love so fulfilling that "those who reach my abode never return to this world" (15.6).

Samadhi – From the word *sam,* "complete," *samadhi* literally means "the complete equality of all things." This is a stage of yogic progress in which the practitioner has completely stilled the fluctuations of the mind and has reached a steady awareness of divinity in all creation. As commonly understood, *samadhi* has two stages: *samprajnata-samadhi*, in which the yogi still distinguishes one object from another; and *asamprajnata-samadhi* (also known as *nirvikalpa-samadhi*), in which the yogi no longer discerns differences of any kind. The Gita uses the word *samadhi* to refer to a steady vision of the Supreme Person everywhere (2.53, 5.18, and 6.24–33).

Sankhya – Common sense dictates that if someone does something, that someone is the "doer" of the action. *Sankhya* doctrine says otherwise, and what it says is endorsed by Krishna. *Sankhya*, considered the oldest of India's six schools of classical philosophy, says there are two categories of energy: consciousness, or souls (*purusha*), and material nature (*prakriti*). Souls are eternal, cognizant, and unchanging. Matter is temporary, inert, and constantly changing under the influence of three qualities (*gunas*): goodness, passion, and ignorance (also defined as balance, expansion, and resistance). When souls forget their eternal nature and incarnate in a material body, they wrongly identify with that body. The soul then thinks, "I am this body" and consequently "I will do things to make life as comfortable as possible for me-the-body." Misidentification with the body leads the soul to wrongly think it is performing actions in the world, when actually (according to *sankhya*) everything in this world is an interaction of the *gunas*. By study and reflection, the soul can emerge from that wrong impression and begin to act again as an eternal being.

Sannyasa – Traditional Indian culture encourages people to retire from work and family life by age sixty or so and cultivate higher consciousness in preparation for death. After retirement some people may choose to enter the formal order of renunciation, called *sannyasa*. Literally "to throw it all down," the renounced order of life is meant to facilitate the throwing down of all the needs and wishes of this life in order to pursue self-realization full-time. Where should they throw them? "Onto me," Krishna says (3.30), not to escape bothersome responsibility but to take up the higher responsibility of teaching spiritual life to others. *Sannyasa* is not a requirement for achieving full self-realization, but my teacher Prabhupada made clear it can sure help.

Supersoul – see Paramatma.

Varnashrama – *Varnashrama*, improperly understood to mean "caste system," originally referred to four general divisions of labor (*varnas*) and four stages of social life (*ashrams*) required for the upkeep of society. The *varnas* are *shudras,* workers and artists; *vaishyas,* merchants, farmers, and business people; *kshatriyas,* administrators, military and government officials; and *Brahmins,* clergy and educators. The *ashrams* are *brahmacharis,* celibate students; *grihasthas,* married people; *vanaprasthas,* retired folks; and *sannyasis,* members of the renounced order such as monks, nuns, and others who leave society to completely dedicated themselves to God. The original idea outlined in ancient Sanskrit texts sought to encourage people to pursue vocations and social standing appropriate to their skills, abilities, and psychic disposition. The corrupted version seeks to isolate and control populations by arbitrarily declaring that only someone born into a brahmin family can be a brahmin and those born in outcaste families remain outcaste throughout life—essentially distorting the original concept for political ends.

Vedas – The Vedas are scriptural user's manuals for living in the material world. The Supreme Person communicated the original Veda into the heart of Brahma, first being of the universe, who divided them into four. The *Rig-Veda* contains 1,028 hymns addressed to various gods. The *Sama-Veda* is a selection of verses from the *Rig-Veda* with musical instructions for their proper recitation. The *Yajur-Veda* is a book of Vedic ceremonies, with verses and prose for use by priests who perform the manual part of the sacrifices. The *Atharva-Veda* consists of spells and incantations. The Vedas offer no histories or doctrines (which are found in the supplementary texts) but concern themselves exclusively with details for the offering of sacrifice (*yajna*) that formed the core of the Vedic religion. Tradition maintains that, while the Vedas may have been compiled at a particular date in history, the knowledge they contain is eternal and appears in each new creation.

Yoga – The word yoga and its variations appear nearly 150 times in the Gita. The root *yuj* means to yoke as the yoking of horses to a chariot. Yoga is the "yoking" or reuniting of the individual soul with the Supreme Soul. To achieve this reuniting, a person can employ various tools such as asana practice (*ashtanga-yoga*, also called *raja-yoga*), study of scripture and contemplation (*jnana-yoga*) and selfless action (*karma-yoga*). Krishna states that the highest goal is love for him and that the best tool for reawakening this love is *bhakti*, or loving devotional service.

RECOMMENDED READINGS

Readers might find the following books rewarding. Each has its particular merits.

THE BHAGAVAD GITA AND COMMENTARIES:

A.C. Bhaktivedanta Swami Prabhupada
Bhagavad Gita As It Is
(Los Angeles: Bhaktivedanta Book Trust, 1971)
This work by the preeminent bhakti guru provides original Sanskrit verses, transliterations, word-for-word translations, and elaborate purports. Since the 1970s, this has been the world's most popular edition of the Gita. The publisher has made it available in various sizes including a convenient pocket edition.

Steven J. Rosen, ed.
Holy War: Violence & The Bhagavad Gita
(Hampton, VA: Deepak Heritage Books, 2002).
Here is a fascinating collection of essays exploring various interpretations of the Gita's position on violence, nonviolence, and the meaning of a "holy war."

Graham Schweig
Bhagavad Gita: The Beloved Lord's Secret Love Song
(San Francisco: HarperSanFrancisco, 2007)
Scholar-practitioner Schweig's edition offers a brief but

insightful introduction, English translation of the verses, followed by the original Sanskrit. My favorite part is the appendix titled "Textual Illuminations," a highly readable analysis of the Gita's secret, more secret, and most secret teachings.

Eric J. Sharpe,
The Universal Gita: Western Images of the Bhagavad Gita
(La Salle, IL: Open Court Publishing, 1985)
No better work is available on the history of the Gita in the West beginning with its first translation into English by Charles Wilkins in 1785. Sharpe traces the Gita's influence on the Transcendentalists, Gandhi, Rudolf Otto, T.S. Elliott, and others.

THE MAHABHARATA:

William Buck
Mahabharata
(New York, London: Meridian, 1987)
This is an exciting literary rendering, poetic and sensitive, although Buck took liberties with the original to achieve his version.

The Mahabharata
(DVD, Image Entertainment)
This is a filmed adaptation of the stage production written by Jean-Claude Carrière and directed by former Royal Shakespeare Company director Peter Brook. This multinational production is more about Brook's theatrical acumen than the original story, but its six-hour running time moves quickly thanks to Carrière's superb script and Brook's inventive staging.

Kamala Subramaniam
The Mahabharata
(Mumbai: Bharatiya Vidya Bhavan, 2007)
Perhaps the most popular version of the epic available in
English, this book has been through fourteen printings
since its initial publication in 1965. It reads easily and
conveys all the key elements of the Sanskrit original.

OTHER RECOMMENDED READINGS:

A.C. Bhaktivedanta Swami Prabhupada,
KRSNA: The Supreme Personality of Godhead
(Los Angeles: Bhaktivedanta Book Trust, 1970)

ACKNOWLEDGMENTS

his book began as a handout for students at Hofstra University and Jivamukti Yoga School, so my acknowledgements begin with them for keeping me immersed in Gita wisdom. Raoul Goff at Mandala Publishing suggested others might appreciate reading an expanded version of that handout, and here we are. Raoul is a beacon of light in the publishing world, and he deserves deepest appreciation for his important work.

The manuscript benefited from scathing comments by scholar-practitioner Jayadvaita Swami. My thanks to him as well as to the following for their review and suggestions: editors Kaisori devi dasi and Vishakha devi dasi, author and publisher Steve Rosen (Satyaraj das), Religions for Peace consultant Vineet Chander (Vyenkata Bhatta das), interfaith pioneer Rukmini Walker (who wisely combined both her names), distinguished yoga instructor Beth Krafchik, Sanskritist Paul Sherbow, and to the many other friends and colleagues who offered valuable input.

The wonderful people at Mandala Publishing deserve special mention for their support and good cheer, particularly managing editor Jake Gerli, editor Lucy Kee, and creative director Iain Morris.

Funding for the year of writing *Gita Wisdom* was generously provided by my life partner Esther, a frequent underwriter of my work, who rightfully asks when it will all end. I have suggested she consult Chapter 2 verses 13-17.

A NOTE ABOUT THE ILLUSTRATIONS

The illustrations included in this book are by the
great modern Indian masters B.G. Sharma and Indra
Sharma. Their artwork is explored in more detail and
reproduced in full color in these other titles from
Mandala Publishing:

Form of Beauty: The Krishna Art of B.G. Sharma
with text by Swami B.V. Tripurari

*In a World of Gods and Goddesses:
The Mystic Art of Indra Sharma*
with text by James H. Bae

The main type was set in Adobe Caslon.
The footnote type was set in Warnock Pro Light.
The display type was set in Poetica.